D1368491

Web Traffic Magnet - 55 free things you can do to drive traffic to your website

Contents

Introduction

Welcome to *Web Traffic Magnet - 55 free things you can do to drive traffic to your website*.

This book is for anyone who wants to know why traffic is not coming to their website and who is looking for practical ways of solving the problem that cost little or no money.

Even if you do a *fraction* of the action items in this book, you will increase traffic to your website. What's more, this is all about driving more of the *right* traffic to your website – people who are looking for what you offer, but have never heard about you – not just traffic for its own sake.

There are actually more than 55 Action Items in this book, but I am only counting the 55 that can be done without spending money.

Where explanation is needed, each topic is discussed and then the related Action Item follows. Each Action Item is printed in a gray box with a border and a shadow.

> # 1 This is what an action item looks like.

You can browse through all of the action items in a few minutes to get an idea of how easy most of it is to do. With the exception of Google Analytics, you should be able to bounce back and forth through the book as takes your fancy.

Some Action Items might on the surface appear to contradict each other. For example, in one item I recommend modeling your SEO Target Pages to reflect your business structure, while another item recommends you model them to reflect your prospect types. Each method has been seen to be effective and I wanted to include methods my customers found to be effective, not just what I personally have tried.

Search Engine Optimization is about making search engines understand what is on your website, and everything in this book is about making that happen for your website. I don't have any fancy tricks or ways to "game the system", but I explain how to put everything in place so that **when someone is looking for what your business is offering, they find you.**

Death of Interrupt Marketing; Birth of Inbound Marketing

2008: We are experiencing the death of interrupt marketing. Instead of responding to telemarketing calls when we sit down to dinner, or filtering the one-in-a-thousand interesting items from our junk mail, we purchasers are turning to the Internet to find what we need. In fact, 40% of all consumer spending begins today with a web search and a staggering 85% of business-to-business transactions begin there. So if your website doesn't appear early in search results, you lose business.

This book is a collection of my own tried-and-tested methods, blog entries, advice to and from dozens of customers, conversations with fellow experts and the result of fourteen years of experience developing solutions on the Internet. I've coded shopping carts, e-commerce solutions, credit card handling routines and developed one of the earliest web traffic analysis products in the mid-1990s. I have distilled it all down to a set of actionable items explained in a way that anyone will understand. You don't have to be technical; this is an easy read and I explain everything as I go.

When you apply the information here to your own website, you will have a profound effect on its traffic. Some of the action items will take effect more quickly than others, but even after reading the table of contents, you'll probably want to check your website.

I've crammed as much into as few pages as possible. This allows me to keep the book price reasonable. Adding page breaks to the beginning of chapters would have added about a dollar to the price, so I took them out.

I wish you all the best of success. Email me if you have a question or would like to talk. My contact details are on page 62 and I'd love to hear from you.

Liam Scanlan
August 2008

Inbound Links pay you back in three ways

What is an Inbound Link?

An Inbound Link is a link from outside one of your web pages in to that web page. For example, a link on a page of IBM's website to a page on my website would be an Inbound Link. The page containing the link must be visible to search engines in order for it to be "counted". (In other words, a link from inside an intranet would not be considered an Inbound Link of value, because search engines cannot see it).

The three ways an Inbound Link helps your website

1. Short term: as soon as you make a posting to, for example, a popular forum on the Internet you will likely get some immediate traffic to your website over the first hours and days your blog posting is in existence. Readers (capital "R" for automated Readers that pick up changes on a website and inform subscribers that a page has changed) let people know immediately that something new has arrived and they go look at it.

2. Medium term: Over the following weeks and months, stragglers trolling the Internet stumble into your website by following the link to your website.

3. Long term: In many cases, an Inbound Link will live for years, perhaps decades. In most cases, each surviving Inbound Link is counted to support your Google PageRank (PageRank is explained on page 93) which will benefit you for years to come. This is what they call the "long tail" effect. For good or bad, stuff that happens on the Internet sometimes lasts for a very long time indeed.

An Inbound Link from a page with a higher PageRank is worth more than an Inbound Link from a page with a lower PageRank.

Consider a link to your web page a "vote" by the originating page. If that originating page has earned "100 points", those 100 points are divided equally among all five of the pages being linked to from that page. By the way, such links do not affect the PageRank of the originating page. (Some people call this a "vote"; the vote is divided up among all the web pages a page links to.)

Let's say you secured a link from the page www.ici.ie/index.shtml to your own website. If there were a total of five links (including the link to your website) from that *page*, the value of the link to your web *page* is divided by five.

1.When hunting for opportunities to secure Inbound Links from other web pages to one of your own web pages, remember that the more outbound links from a page, the less valuable each outbound link is to the page it links to. Before you put too much work on someone else's site into a potential Inbound Link back to one of your web pages, get a quick idea of the number of outbound links that page has, and go for the pages with fewer outbound links on them if you have a choice. All else being equal, they are worth more to you, because they contribute more to your own PageRank.

Keeping your postings brief

Brevity is the soul of wit
— **William Shakespeare, Hamlet**

Unless you are Brad Pitt or Paris Hilton, chances are your readers don't want to hear how your day is going, what the weather is like where you live or at what time you awoke this morning. They want to hear something new and valuable about your subject matter.

Blog postings should be short and sweet. If they are long, and I admit I like to get into detail myself sometimes, there should be plenty of relevant material present. Each paragraph should have something valuable and relevant to the subject in it.

In this regard, a good blog posting might start like "The best way to keep knitting needles from rusting is to keep them in ziplock bags containing desiccants....".

A poor blog posting might begin "Now that I've had my second cup of coffee, I am ready to start my first blog posting of the day...".

2.Start, continue and wrap up every blog posting on subject.

It's not just about Keywords

Keywords are definitely important to get right, both in the body of content on your website and the Keyword metatags themselves (see page 59 for a full description). You need to know what search words people use on the Internet when they are looking for the products or services you offer. There is another big element to Keyword matching that many people forget, or perhaps, they simply do not have the time, money or desire to invest in it: *A Preponderance of Relevant Content.*

A Preponderance of Relevant Content

Google doesn't only take the words a person enters in search and try to match them directly against Keywords that have been found on web pages. Google also has a record of words that are *semantically related* to the search words entered by the person doing the search. For example, when a person searches for "wooden chair", Google might find a match using related words, like seat, or bench.

To understand the significance of semantically related content, try this experiment:

3.At the URL: http://labs.google.com/sets, enter the words **sofa**, **couch** and **bench**, then click the "small set" button. Google will display a list of words that have something in common with the words you entered. Google knows that "when a web page contains *these* words, it often also contains these *other* words". When you first decide on your own Keywords for your web page, run them through Google Sets to discover, at least according to Google, their semantically related words.

See the section on Google Sets on page 42 for more detail.

When you are blogging on your subject, use semantically related words in addition to your Keywords. Over time, Google will see that your website doesn't just contain the exact search words entered by the searching person, but is talking all over the subject the search words relate to.

That will give you a higher MatchScore than the Keywords on their own. See page 40 for a description of MatchScore.

Using Google Analytics to monitor progress

It sounds scary, but Google Analytics is easy to use to examine what's happening on your website. All you need to do is paste a few lines of HTML, which Google provides to you, into any of your own web pages for which you want to monitor traffic.

If the pages of your website are all based on a "master" page or a "template" or if you use a Web Content Management System (like Drupal or Big Medium™) you might be able to add those few lines of HTML into the top level template for your website. That washes down to every page in your website. Ask your website person about helping you do that.

Google Analytics is simple, elegant, valuable and free.

How does Google Analytics work?

The few lines of code, when executed by the browser when a person visits one of your web pages, send a signal to the Google Analytics server to say "hey dude, someone just looked at this page!" Google Analytics then stores all this data with all the other visits to the page – as well as your whole website – and uses it to construct different graphs (like how many visitors, where they originated, etc.). After only a few days of people looking at your website, you can log into Google Analytics and see the charts for your website. It's just like you might create a chart in Excel with a table of data, but Google does the work for you. Once you've used Google Analytics once, you'll wonder how you ever survived without it. Google Analytics is free.

Strangers can't view your Google Analytics charts because they can't log in to your Google Analytics account, and they can't insert their own Google Analytics HTML into your web page because they can't change your web pages either.

Google Analytics is a great way to find out which Keywords are working and which are not.

Google Analytics shows you such things as how many unique visitors you get every day, what % of them visit only one page then go away (called the "bounce rate"), what search words visitors used to get there if they did a search, and a bunch of other stuff. It's a great way to check how effective your new search words are.

Google Analytics is a great way to find out which Inbound Links are sending you the most traffic.

Search for "Google Analytics" and sign up for the service. It will walk you through the steps of getting the HTML you need to add to your web pages. It will also tell you where exactly to add them.

Google Analytics is a great way to find out which of your blog postings are generating the most visits.

4.Visit www.google.com/analytics and sign up for a Google Analytics account. Follow the instructions, which involves copying/pasting a few lines of Google Analytics HTML code into your own web pages. After a few days have passed, return to Google Analytics to see your traffic reports.

Post at the same time every day

This is just a guess, but when your website is eventually checked by search engines every day, it will probably be done at roughly the same time every day. In any case, it is better to assume that it is, rather than it is not, done at the same time every day.

Let's assume for the moment that search engines do, in fact, check your website at the same time of the day. If it is true, your postings to the website are best spaced 24 hours apart so that every day, a change is noticed by a given search engine. If search engines scan your site at an effectively random time of the day, then it won't hurt to make your blog posting at the same time every day.

If Tuesday's posting were published at 6pm (on Tuesday) and Wednesday's posting was published at 4am (Wednesday), and if a search engine indexes your website at noon every day, both postings might look like a single change at noon on Wednesday, and no change would present on the day before – which was Tuesday – because Tuesday's posting was published too late in the day to get picked up by the noon scan by the search engine. Phew. A bit long-winded, I know.

It's like taking out the trash. If trash collection occurs every Friday morning, putting it out at the same time every week is the way to maximize your use of the service.

> # 5.Make at least one significant change to your website every day and if possible, at the same time every day. If you are using a Content Management System to control the contents of your website, use its scheduling feature to control when each piece of new material is published on the website.

Nine common web mistakes

Embedding Flash in home page

The worst example is when home page designers embed the link to the main website right inside the Flash object. This is a link that the search engines cannot follow.

If it is a one-page website or a website where you don't want the search engines to index anything, then it is fine. (Like a website that is so temporary that there won't even be time for the search engines to crawl over it).

Keep Flash for pages from which links are not important. Your home page is probably your most important page - it is the one that usually receives the highest search engine rankings because it is the center of your website and the page with the shortest URL.

6.Make sure any important links inside your Flash animation also exist outside the Flash Animation in the same page. For example, if you have a link to your product page, make sure the link is also included outside the Flash animation. This allows search engines to find, in this example, the products page.
(As of July 2008, Google can read links embedded in Flash animations, but many other search engines probably cannot).

Flash menus in home page

Although this also may change in the future, Flash menus on your website are not indexable[1] by search engines. Links inside them cannot be deciphered by search engines, so the pages they reference are invisible to search engines. There has been some talk about Google – this is July 2008 – working on a solution to this issue also – so by the time you read this, it might not be true any longer, at least for Google.

Simple HTML links from one page to another are better for search engines than links from inside Flash menus or other objects. Alternatively, use small images with links from them to the page of choice, making sure you include an Alt Text (Alt Text is described on page 23) with each image so the search engines know what the image is about and what the page being linked to is about.

7.Make sure all links within Flash menus are also included elsewhere on the same page – so that search engines can see them.

---

[1] Indexable: A web page is indexable when search engines can comb through a page and determine its contents, particularly embedded links to other pages.

Images where text should be used

Embed images in your web pages for graphical illustration only. Use text for any content which you would like search engines to pick up.

Some websites display textual content inside images, which search engines cannot read. Always use an Alt Text value to describe what is in the image, and make sure the file name of the image says something about the contents.

8.Replace with text all images that contain only text. For example, if your company's telephone number is contained in an image, remove the image from your website and place the phone number in a text box. Sometimes the only material someone has to find you on the web is a phone number, and you want search engines to be able to see that phone number on your website.

Using AJAX without equivalent links

AJAX is a method of mixing the two "languages" of XML and JavaScript. It stands for Asynchronous JavaScript and XML – a term to be used strictly at cocktail parties only – allowing partial refreshes of web pages.

AJAX allows websites to refresh small sections of a web page without having to refresh the whole web page like websites had to do only a few years ago. This gives the user a superior, faster experience of the online program and reduces the burden on the website server delivering the data because the server is being asked to do less work. Anyone who is familiar with Gmail – or any other sophisticated web application – knows how convenient it is when only a section of a page is refreshed, instead of having to refresh the entire web page. AJAX makes that possible.

The problem is search engines find it almost impossible to find links within AJAX, because to get to those links, a user would have to interact with the AJAX in the web page. For example, if you could only see the contents of the Order History page after you had entered a customer number, search engines would never see the Order history page. Search engines can't do that because they don't have a customer number and have no real way of mimicking the sequence of entries made on a web page.

9.This only applies if your website uses AJAX. If you're not sure, ask your webmaster if it is so. Make sure links embedded in pages served by AJAX are also available elsewhere on the page, that is, if you want the pages they reference to be found by search engines. A small box at the bottom of the page listing the links would be fine.

Changing page names (URLs)

Keep page names static. (See example of a web page name, two paragraphs below). Once you have created a page, leave its page name as it is, giving search engines enough time to index it and time for Inbound Links to accumulate, age and grow in value.

10.It is generally believed – for no one outside Google truly knows any of this stuff for a fact – Inbound Links that have been around for a while have a greater positive influence on a page's Google PageRank than new Inbound Links do. It's just like adding to a high interest savings account – the earlier you start investing, the better – so get cracking on generating Inbound Links as soon as you can, and keep the URLs of the pages they point to unchanged forever.

Look at how most newspapers build their websites and you will see many good examples of page name preservation in action. Here is an example of a page on the Guardian newspaper website in the UK:

http://www.guardian.co.uk/world/gallery/2008/may/30/brazil.photography

The URL is constructed to preclude the possibility of a duplicate URL being used in the future. As the Guardian newspaper accumulates more and more news items, the sheer bulk of their content, as well as the persistence of their pages, makes their website very attractive to search engines. They have over a million Inbound Links to their website. No surprise, then, that the Google PageRank for their home page is a whopping 9 out of 10. (See "Sharecropper..." on page 31 for more information about the risks of Inbound Links.)

Using a Content Management System – like Big Medium from GlobalMoxie.com or the open source program Drupal both of which output search engine friendly web pages – is a great way to keep your content indexable by Google.

11.If you must change the URLs of your web pages as you change content, keep the older pages, and keep a link to each of those old pages from somewhere within your website so that search engines can continue to find them.

Not using Anchor Text in an Inbound Link

Anchor text is the text you see displayed "over" a link.

Here is an example of a link *without* Anchor Text. It gives no hint as to the contents of the destination website:

http://www.ici.ie

In contrast, the following link uses Anchor Text:

Executive Life Coaching Services

You can see that the second example gives information about the probable content of the page to which the link points.

Links with Anchor Text from other websites to yours are more valuable than links without Anchor Text. By telling the search engines about the content of your website, they reinforce your website's "ownership" of the subject.

12.Always use *Anchor Text with subject-reinforcing words* and not just a simple link back to your website when creating Inbound Links back to your site from elsewhere. Most importantly, Anchor Text tells search engines what your website is about and increases your chances of getting a higher MatchScore. See page 40 for a full description of MatchScore.

Meaningless Title Tags

Things to consider when writing the title tag:

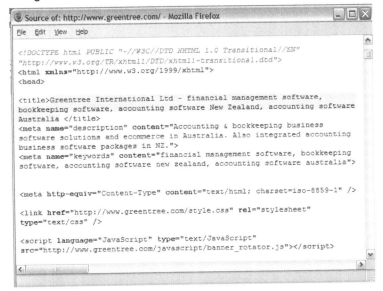

Figure 1 - Example of a good title tag (highlighted in HTML)

Ideally, the company name would NOT come first, but otherwise it is a good example of a title tag done well.

13.Make sure the contents of the Title Tag on each important page of your website contains text that supports your Keywords. Avoid text like "Products Page" or "picture of a dog" or any other generic words that are unlikely to be entered as search words by a would-be customer. Example of a potentially effective Title Tag that supports search words potential customers might use: "Deep Sea Fishing Rods".

Not using Alternate Text

"Alt Text" means Alternate Text and it was "attached" to an image on a web page when the image was added to the page. Its original purpose, by the way, was as an alternative to displaying an image on a page when, due to bandwidth constraints, the image could not be displayed. When an image could not be displayed or was missing, the browser would display the Alt Text in its place.

Today, search engines use Alt Text to determine what is in an image as well as to determine the subject matter of the page it is on.

Alternate text is supplied alongside the reference to the image in HTML. It's always good to have a meaningful Alt text to help search engines determine meaning and context of every image on your website. In other words, the Alt Text should describe the image it is associated with.

Figure 2 – HTML example of Alt text for an image

14. To find out if an image has an alternate text, open the page containing the image in a browser and hold your mouse over the image for a few moments; the text that displays, if any displays, is the Alternate Text.
Use your Content Management System or HTML Editor to add an Alternate Text to every image on your website. Use text that supports your Keywords, for example, "knitting needles for wool socks".

Meaningless URLs

URLs that give no clue as to the content of the page make it less likely the page will achieve a good MatchScore.

The following link gives the reader a sense of what the document is about and it helps the search engines deliver search results that more closely match what the searching person is looking for:

http://www.greenroadtech.com/documents/fuel-consumption.pdf

Six ways to improve Page Titles

Have a different title tag for each page

15.If each page on your website has the same title tag, search engines will view them as having a similar purpose. It is better that each page attracts different web searches. Make a note of the title of each page on your website (the title is in the top bar of the page when you open the page in a browser) and change each of them to be unique.

Include your Keywords for each page in its title

16.The Title Tag is the most important factor in deciding if search words match the page. Incorporate the most important words on a page into the title of the page. For example, "Fishing Rods, bait, boots and other tackle from Joe's Supplies" where **fishing**, **tackle** and **bait** are the Keywords for the page.

Place most important Keywords at the beginning

17.Make sure the most important Keyword is at the *beginning* of the Title Tag. "Lighting services from Acme in Seattle" is better than "Acme lighting services, Seattle" because you want people who don't yet know your company name to find you, so put the most likely search words first. Don't use your company name in the page title and avoid words like "Welcome" - something a prospect is unlikely to enter into search – in your page Title Tag.

Keep Page Titles short

18. The Title tag for each page should be shorter than about 65 characters. I've also heard ninety-something as the limit; in any case, shorter is better. Anything more than that is usually ignored by search engines and long titles can look a little odd in the top title bar of the browser when someone is visiting the web page that contains it.

Don't overstuff the Title Tag with Keywords

19. Don't stuff the title tag with dozens of Keywords. Keep it short and easy to read. If you need more Keywords to describe what the page is all about, split the page into two or more pages. Keep it limited to seven Keywords in a single page Title Tag.

Avoid duplicate words

20. "Life coaching and other coaching services" repeats the word "coaching". Better to have "Life coaching and related services" or take the opportunity to use a similar word "Life coaching and other counseling services". Use the words you know searching people use.

Securing links from high value sites

An Inbound Link to your site is valuable mostly because it can increase the value of the PageRank of the page it points to, thereby making your page more attractive to Google.

Inbound links are not all of the same value, however. Some are *hundreds of times more valuable* than others. In addition to links to your site being potentially neutralized with the "nofollow" tag (see page 67 for details on the "nofollow" tag), the website they are coming from might have low TrustRank, PageRank and web traffic, each of which will diminish the value of the Inbound Link coming from it.

- TrustRank: determines how "reliable" a website is, according to Google.

- PageRank: a quality ranking for each page on the website, based on many factors – from length of time the domain name has existed (even though the website itself might be brand new) to number of Inbound Links pointing to the site, also according to Google.

- Web Traffic: how many unique visitors (not to be confused with "hits") pass through the page or website in question.

Usually, owners of sites that score highly on the above metrics know that links from their website are worth something, so they will dole out links carefully. Often, you need to have a relationship with them in order for them to agree to have a link from their site. For truly high value sites, consider becoming a regular blogger to their site, with the understanding that each link can contain a link back to your site.

Creating the bulk of high quality Inbound Links takes work and dedication. There are no easy ways to do it and there are no quick-and-easy tools out there that will do it for you, even though many advertise their services as such. It is a particularly important exercise in the early life of your website – when content is more limited and there are few if any links to your website that might drive visitors to it – that you create those first Inbound Links to the site.

> # 21.Follow the money. I have found that Inbound Links from forums or blogs on established business sites (where visitors have money) are an order of magnitude more valuable that those on sites relating to, for example, startups (where visitors have no money). Give postings to established business sites precedence over postings to other sites. For example, the Bank of America Small Business forum instead of a site that might have the words "startup" in it. It will bring a better class of visitor to your site – those with money to spend.

Incurring the wrath of blog owners

The very day before I was about to wrap up my final edits of this book, I had an interesting experience on the web that got me back to the keyboard with one last addition. The experience was about striking a balance between delivering value to another person's website – with a link back to ones own – and lacing the blog posting with self-serving links back to ones own website.

For the past several months, I have been making the odd posting to the forum on one of the many business websites out there. In the past, every time I made a posting to that site, I added one simple link back to my own website. From that perspective, every posting was certainly self-serving – I wanted the inbound link to my website to count towards my own PageRanks – but I always made sure I gave good content value, in the form of interesting and useful information, to anyone who might read the blog posting. Yesterday, the article I posted was a heavily edited version of a posting I had made to my own site several weeks earlier – redacted to fit the specific audience of this online business community. This morning, I thought I would check to see if there were any comments on my posting of yesterday, so I went back to revisit the posting. When I went to log in to their site, I discovered that my account was gone. My login and the entire handful of postings and comments I had made to that forum since I created my account on it had been deleted. I had been fired from the forum!

I inquired as to why – and I have no reply yet – but looking back on it, I can guess that I broke at least one rule they have for contributions. I might have had *several* links back to my site in the one posting. Furthermore, a copy check might have detected sufficient similarities between the posting I made yesterday and the original article on my own website. That might have triggered a flag for lack of originality, even though it was from my very own site.

> # 22. When you post to others' blogs, forums or other online communities, your contribution must be original and unique. That means that the posting does not exist anywhere else on the web, even on your own website. Well-managed websites – those from which Inbound Links are consequently more valuable – check the originality of your posting and may delete your entire account (from their website) if they find a problem.

> # 23. When you make a post to a blog owned by someone else, don't lace it with links back to your website. Rule-of-thumb: Limit links to your own website to one per posting. A blog posting with too many links, especially to your own website, will draw the attention and possible wrath of the website owners, and may result in your account and all of the postings – together with all of your hard-earned Inbound Links from their website – being deleted.

The experience of having my entire account deleted, along with my postings and the half-dozen Inbound Links to my website they contained, was a stark reminder about the value of content. I talk more about this subject in the next chapter, but it is worth noting here that *whoever owns the domain name owns the value.*

Winners and Losers in the Content Game

The winners in the SEO content game are those who own final control of its "container", not those who make the blog postings. In other words, if you own the *domain name* upon which the content resides, you ultimately own the value. To some, this is obvious. To others, it might be an irrelevant subtlety, but this morning, I lost a half dozen high value links to my website at the complete discretion of a stranger. I could have gotten defensive about being kicked off that particular forum, but the fact is, I was a little careless and I paid a price for it.

There is a bigger lesson here, however, than just needing to be more careful about creating Inbound Links, and it leads us into the big subject of the next chapter: The Value and Ownership of Content.

The Value and Ownership of Content

Host your blog where you own the domain name

You may have known for a long time that your business needs a blog. You might have tons of ideas for content and you might even have typed up copious quantities of notes in preparation for your blog ... when you finally get to it, that is.

The question many ask is, where should the blog be hosted?

In order to answer that question, know that whoever owns, and consequently controls, the domain name upon which the blog is located ultimately possesses the value contained in the blog. Moving a blog to a different domain invalidates all the old links into the original, and presents many other challenges.

Whoever owns the domain name of the blog host owns the value contained in the blog.

A blog is valuable when it contains valuable information, has serious traffic and has many Inbound Links pointing to it. If and when your blog ever grows to the point where you have plenty of such postings, and as long as you have control over it, you have a number of options open to you, including placing ads – yours or someone else's – on your blog to generate revenue.

When someone else, either an individual or an organization, owns the domain name on which your blog is hosted, they own - and consequently may decide to control – any downstream revenue opportunities should they decide to exercise that right. That might be perfectly OK with you, and companies like Google – they own the domain name blogspot.com, by the way – are very magnanimous about it, but you should understand that you are "planting trees on another person's land", if you use such a blog hosting service.

Sharecroppers, Serfs and Bloggers

Another way to describe this dilemma is that you are a kind of "Sharecropper". Any scholar of American history will explain to you why you don't want to be a sharecropper. The serfs of old England are another such example of workers being exploited by real estate owners and there are countless others throughout history and religion, from France and Italy to Islamic Law, where landowners let people use their land for a fee in goods, service or monetary compensation. It usually ends in tears.

Being of Irish heritage, I have some anxiety around the notion of someone owning the land upon which I am making a living and I believe today's equivalent of sharecropping and serfdom is bloggers posting to a blog on a domain name owned by someone else.

A professional blog posting might be worth about $100, so consider it a real gift when you post to someone else's blog. Would you buy a tree sapling for $100 and plant it in your neighbor's yard?

It's all about the Domain Name

Some free blogging servers, for example Blogger.com (which uses the domain name blogspot.com to host its blogs), allow you to point a domain name directly at your blog. See illustration in Figure 3 for how Blogger (blogspot.com) allows you to use your own domain name for your blog. This means that your blog can live at, for example www.johnnysblog.com (owned by you), even though you set it up under johnnys-great-dog-blog.blogspot.com (owned by someone else). Even though the blog is hosted under a domain name owned by Google (blogspot.com), all of your references to the blog use the domain name that *you own* (johnnysblog.com). *You own the content* because *you own the domain name* people use to refer to it.

Figure 3 - Using ones own Domain Name in blogger.com

24.As you go hunting for Inbound Links, always point back to URLs, for example http://www.johnnysblog.com/all-about-dogs.html, that are within a domain name that *you own*. Don't use the blogging software hosting company URL (for example http://johnnys-great-dog-blog.blogspot.com/all-about-dogs.html).
At some point in the future, if the owners of the original domain name under the blog ever try to take control of your blog, you can simply move the entire website contents to a hosting company and redirect johnnysblog.com to point to it. You can do that redirect because you own the domain name johnnysblog.com.

Blogging Capability built into the Website

Professionally run businesses use a Content Management System (CMS, or sometimes called a Web Content Management System, WCMS) to manage their website. There are poor CMSs and there are excellent ones, and everything in between. The SiteLeads.net website is managed using a CMS called Big Medium. Like any good CMS, blogging functionality is built into Big Medium. The blog on www.SiteLeads.net is a part of the fundamental structure of the website and it is therefore owned by the organization that owns the domain name SiteLeads.net.

Make sure you or your company owns the domain name upon which your or their blog is hosted.

Look at the domain name of your blog. For example, the blog at http://portfolio-living.blogspot.com/ is owned by the owner of the domain name blogspot.com. Even though I can, for the moment, control the ads I place on that blog, that fact could change in the future; the owners of the domain blogspot.com could change the rules of any advertising hosted on it.

If your blog is central to the value of your company or organization, come acquisition time, not owning the domain upon which it is hosted might lessen the amount you could get for your company, or preclude the acquisition altogether.

If you are posting to a newspaper or other blog, know that the newspaper owns the value you create. They should be grateful. You are "giving them $100" with every posting you make.

25.If it's not too late, make sure your blog is hosted on a domain that you or your company owns. If you or your company does not own the domain name that hosts your blog, consider migrating everything over to a new blog implemented inside your own website. Add a line and link to the end of each blog posting in the old blog – leaving the old blog entries intact – pointing to the equivalent blog posting in your new blog. This is potentially a lot of work, but if your blog is part of your intellectual property, it is worth protecting.
Alternatively, start making posts to a new blog – one hosted on a domain you own – in parallel with the older, more established blog. Focus your Inbound Linking efforts on the new blog going forward.

Having said all that, it is sometimes good blogging practice to make high-value blog posts in your own name to high-value and high-trafficked blogs. This can drive traffic to your own site, which is what you might rely upon in the early stages of your website, but more importantly, it will show that you make good faith contributions to communities interested in your subject.

26.Make the occasional blog posting to others' websites. Each such posting offers the possibility of creating a link back to your website, but more importantly, demonstrates your willingness to offer a good faith contribution to web communities.

Focus on those postings with the highest traffic

For all your best laid plans, you can't always predict which of your blog postings will generate the most traffic.

By now, I am assuming you have taken the time to familiarize yourself with Google Analytics. (If you have not yet done that, return to and follow the instructions on the installation and use of it).

Use Google Analytics to determine which web pages are generating the most inbound traffic, either as a result of Inbound Links or as a result of successful Keyword matching.

Look at the search words that Google Analytics says were used to find each specific page on your website. What do they have in common? Perhaps they have Keywords that are very effective, or content that is compelling. Whatever the reason, rework those high-traffic pages again for clarity, punctuation and grammar. While succinct blog entries are often more desirable than long essay-length ones, adding a little text might still be ok, as long as it is relevant, well written and interesting. It might also help to add images, a spreadsheet or even a sound file or video to support the point you are making in the blog posting.

Consider using the most popular pages as SEO Targeted Landing pages. I.e. the most popular pages on your website might be natural starting points on your website and might be more likely to encourage visitors to continue reading.

"Landing page"; targeting specific pages

Air Traffic Controllers give arriving aircraft pilots a specific runway upon which to land. Thankfully they don't say "you are cleared to land at Denver International" but rather, "you are cleared to land at runway 52". The pilot is given a specific runway upon which to land.

Search Engine Optimization is best served when specific pages are targeted – **SEO Target Pages** – particularly when it comes to creating Inbound Links on other sites that point to your website.

> **# 27.**Make a list of your SEO Target Pages by selecting those that you wish visitors to come to when they perform a search. You can add to the list later, but the first step is to make the list.
>
> Before you make a posting to an external site with a view to adding a link back to your site, decide which of your SEO Target Pages it relates to. The topic of every external posting – with a link back to your website – should relate to the same topic as the page on your website to which it is linked. In other words, if you are in the fishing tackle business and are posting something about metal fishing rods to a fishing hobbyists' blog, include a link back to a specific page on your website that talks about metal fishing rods.

What makes a good SEO Target Page?

Many businesses have several distinct customer types. A cosmetic surgeon might do facelifts for one type of customer and post-cancer reconstructive surgery for another. A legal services company might do family law for one customer type and human resources for another. Each customer type will use different search words, so having a target page focused on each type of service, heavily optimized to attract related search words, increases the chances that each page will appear earlier in search results.

It is better to have a single page (from your website) appear on the first page of search results, than to have ten of your pages appear on page seven of search results.

Even if you have hundreds of pages on your website, two or three pages may stand above the rest for their greater quality, interest or web traffic. A high value page might relate to one of your best-selling or most profitable products, or it might be an outstanding endorsement from a happy customer. True, all pages do contribute to the overall quality of your website, as well as TrustRank and PageRank of the home page, but it is individual pages that are listed in search results, not websites.

> # 28. Make sure every Inbound Link you create back to your site points to a specific page on your website you have decided will be one of your select SEO Target Pages. Keep the list of pages to which you create Inbound Links as short as possible. This intensifies the importance of a few pages.

Keywords: Hot, Cold or Just Right

Some Keywords are in use by so many people that trying to get traffic to your site by using them is challenging.

Imagine you owned and operated a local bakery. The word "bread" might appear to be an obvious Keyword to build a Keyword strategy round. Alone, the word "bread" is unlikely to attract attention because it is a commonly used word. "Bread" would be considered a "hot" Keyword.

Be specific

If your bakery is based in a suburb of Seattle and sells organic, gluten-free bread, you can create some Keywords (personally, I prefer the term "key phrases" to "Keywords") that result in far fewer pages being found when someone searches using them, giving your web page a better chance of being noticed.

If your Keywords were "organic gluten-free bread, gluten-free bread, gluten-free, Seattle, Bellevue", your page will more likely be picked up for people searching for exactly what you sell.

Perhaps obvious to some, Figure 4 illustrates the narrowing of search results as search words become more specific.

search words	pages found
"bread"	117,000,000
"gluten-free bread"	500,000
"gluten-free bread Seattle"	66,000

"gluten-free bread Seattle Bellevue"	7,000

Figure 4 – example of Keywords and resulting page counts

When there are fewer search results, you stand a better chance of being seen, if of course your website is in the smaller number of search results.

The more closely your content matches the search words, the better your MatchScore will be, and the higher the likelihood your page will appear on the first page of search results.

There are fewer searches against the term "gluten-free bread Seattle Bellevue" than "gluten-free bread", because the latter will pick up the former set of pages *plus* many pages that do not include the Keywords "Seattle" or "Bellevue".

Prospect Type = SEO Target Page

For the purposes of this book, a *prospect type* is defined by the problem a searching person is trying to solve. If your business sells bicycles and also bicycle repair services, consider that to be two customer types because, for a given potential transaction, a prospect is *either* trying to buy a bicycle or looking for bicycle repair services. That means they are usually *searching* for one or the other, which is why you need a separate SEO Target Page for each type of search; one for bicycle sales and another for bicycle repairs.

In my SiteLeads.net business, I have two prospect types: (1) those who want to build a website using a Content Management System and (2) those that are looking for a company to create SEO content for their website. Thus, I have an SEO Target Page for each of those two prospect types. Each of the two SEO Target Pages is heavily linked to the other, so when a prospect arrives who wants both services, either of the SEO Target Pages can take them to the other. But every prospect begins with a search for one of my two services.

29. Make a list of your prospect types. For each, there will be an SEO Target Page. For example, if your business offered tree-trimming, lawn services and driveway restoration as three distinct services, each of those three services should have its own web page – in other words, don't cram all three into a single page that talks about all your services – and each of the three pages should become an SEO Target Page in its own right.

It is tempting to keep descriptions of all three services in a single page, but when a page is focused on a specific prospect type, that page will get a higher MatchScore when that exact prospect type does a search.

The same principle applies to a product company. SEO Target Pages are first determined by prospect type, regardless of the product or service you offer them.

Using Trial-and-error to refine Keywords

You can spend a lot of time trying to figure out exactly which Keywords people use to find your site. And SEO service companies will relieve you of your cash to help you do it. There is a more effective way, however, that involves a little trial and error: Keep adding content page-by-page, and use Google Analytics to see which pages, which Inbound Links and which Keywords are driving the most traffic.

Create a preponderance of content relating to your subject and let Google do the rest.

When you make relevant, useful and succinct postings to your blog every day, you are creating just that preponderance of relevant content. That is what Google and other top notch search engines will match against the search words entered.

A preponderance of content related to the search words will achieve a higher MatchScore than a solid match against Keywords alone.

Understand the role of MatchScore

What is "MatchScore"?

MatchScore measures how closely search words entered match a given web page. I don't know if Google uses that exact term – not that it matters – the important thing is its meaning. I use the word "MatchScore" to help me understand and explain the search process.

*Search words entered by the searching person are compared to the content of **pages**, not **websites**.*

MatchScore is calculated at the time the searching person is looking for something. (Unlike PageRank, which is calculated when Google scans a web page at its own convenience). PageRank is independent of search words and is calculated *per page*. MatchScore is calculated per page, *per search*. You can't see, feel or smell MatchScore. You only know that a page has gotten a relatively high one when it appears in first place in search results.

Example: A searching person types the words "life coaching dublin" into Google search and the following web page scores a very high MatchScore because the words are (a) in its URL (the web address itself), (b) in its Title Tag (displays at the top of browser when you view the page) and (c) throughout the page's content:

http://www.dublin.ie/health/life-coaching.htm

For argument's sake, the MatchScore might be A- for the search words "life coaching dublin".

If the user had typed "life coaching stockholm", the same web page might only score a D+ because one of the three search words, "Stockholm", did not appear anywhere on the page.

If the user had entered "plastic fishing nets", that same web page might score an F (for Fail) and appear nowhere in search results for those search words. No doubt, some other web page would have, justifiably, gotten a high MatchScore for "plastic fishing nets".

Search engines work out how closely each of the billions of pages on the web matches the search words entered by the searching person, and produce **MatchScore**. Of course, search engines have many fancy ways of not having to check every darn page on the 'net every time a search is requested, but the effect is the same; the better the search words match the content on a web page, the more valuable the search engine is to its customers.

Search engines aren't in the business of dark magic. Their interests are well served when people find exactly what they are looking for. Making it easier for search engines to find you helps them deliver better value to their customers.

Make sure phone numbers are not "hidden" in images

Sometimes a phone number is used to find a website

Is your business's telephone number displayed on your website as an image?

People looking for your website will sometimes use your phone number to find it. If your business's phone number was handed from one person to another, which might be the only way your new prospect has of finding you.

Your business's telephone number may get handed from one person to another, but without your business name or even personal name.

Search engines don't know what an image contains. If the contact telephone number on your website (you do have your telephone number on your website, right?) is displayed as an image, make sure its Alt Text contains the phone number. Search engines pick up Alt Texts and use them to create a Keyword match with the image.

Experiment: Use Google to search for your business's telephone number. Does your website display in first page of search results?

Avoiding duplicate content

Search engines have become more adept at discovering web pages that are identical, especially when they are within the same website.

The value of a website is measured partly by the sheer mass of content within a website. One could be forgiven for thinking that by duplicating a few pages, one could "bulk up" the content.

Not so.

It is obviously OK to link to the same page from two different places on the same website - search engines correctly count the destination page as a single page - but duplicating the page is not considered to be good practice and should be avoided.

Latent Semantic Content reinforces Keyword matching

We already know that Keyword density plays a role in a page scoring high on Keyword matching when people search the web for products or services like yours. But what about synonyms? Does Google know when you enter the word "chair", it should also look for "seat" or "bench"?

The answer is, Yes. Words with a similar meaning play a significant role. They help a web page to be found by persons searching with related words and they reinforce a website's "ownership" of a topic.

Latent Semantic Content means words and terms commonly used when talking on the same subject, but which are not the exact Keywords used on a web page.

For example, the website www.boenandgill.com's Keywords might be "fashion handbag" and "designer handbag" and "designer jewelry", but its owners also want to use words and terms that are associated with their set of core Keywords.

There is more on Google Sets on page 42, but for the moment, try this experiment: Visit Google Sets, a little known function that provides a larger set of terms relating to a few you enter. (Search for "Google Sets" – see next Action Item box). Type the three Keywords above, and you will get an interesting list of related terms:

designer handbag

fashion handbag

designer jeans

shoes store

wedding dress

designer clothes

designer purses

designer shoes

clothing store

designer wedding dresses

handbag designers

fashion accessory

As search engines pick up the use of these terms throughout the content on a website, in addition to core Keywords, an "ownership" of the subject is perceived. This increases Keyword matching (MatchScore) and makes it more likely the web page will appear earlier in search results.

30.Visit the URL Google Sets. (In July 2008, it was at labs.google.com/sets). Enter the three to six words you believe visitors are currently using to find your website. Click the "large set" below the entry fields. Note the extended set of terms that is displayed and consider using them in your content creation. See Figure 5.

Figure 5 - an example of Google Sets

Google's process for choosing who appears on Page One

MatchScore, PageRank and search results position

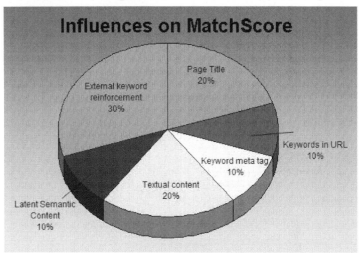

Figure 6 - % share of influences on MatchScore

Only Google knows the exact weighting they apply to each factor that influences which pages appear on page one of search results, and which do not. That process is a jealously guarded secret of course, but by "reading the tealeaves", I've worked out a model that at least fits the facts closely.

Google's first pass is to calculate a score for how closely each page matches the search words entered by the person looking for something. Google then takes the web pages with the highest score and displays them in PageRank order (highest PageRank first).

The process

Search words are received by Google after a person types them into the Google search page and presses Enter.

The words are compared to the entries in an enormous Google database of Keywords associated with hundreds of millions of web pages Google has examined already, resulting in what I call a "MatchScore". (I am not sure what term Google uses internally, if indeed they use any). MatchScore is calculated by awarding points out of a hundred. There are a half-dozen factors that make up 100 points (or percent if you prefer). It's very much like doing a paper at school; to score well, you must try to scoop up at least the easy points on every question.

1. **Page Title: 20 points**. If the search words match the page title exactly, you get most if not all of these points. The looser the match, the fewer points awarded.
    If the search words are "Seattle Light and Power", and the page's Keywords are "lights in Seattle", you might score 15 points out of the available 20.
    The very first words, especially the *first* word, in the page title are the most important; if your page title is "Seattle Plumber and Plumbing Services while-you-wait" and the search words are "Seattle Plumber" you might score the full 20 points.
    If no words match the page title, you get 0 points for this part of it.

2. **Keywords in URL: 10 points**. You score points when the search words match the words in the domain name. If the search words were "life coach Dublin", and your domain name were www.lifecoachdublin.com, you might scoop up most if not all of the available 10 points.
    If you were in the plumbing business in Denver and your domain name was "www.acmecompany.com", search words of "plumber in Denver" would score 0 from the available 10 points.
    If you had a URL on your website like this http://www.acmecompany.com/Denver/plumbing-services.html, you might score 5 (half of the available 10)

points because the search words are at least somewhere in the full page name.

3. **Words in Keyword meta tag: 10 points**: If your Keywords match the search words, you score points. (Search for the text string '<META NAME="Keywords" CONTENT=' in your source code to see your Keywords).

   Too many Keywords will dilute the effectiveness of the Keywords you really want people to gravitate towards. Five to seven Keywords is the ideal range.

   Keywords are actually "key phrases". A Keyword can have several words in it. For example, "Seattle plumbing" and "plumbing in Seattle" are two Keywords.

   It is necessary to separate Keywords using commas, otherwise search engines may consider them to be all the one Keyword, or at best, a list of individual Keywords even though you entered them as phrases. So, Keywords "Seattle plumbing, plumbing in Seattle" are two distinct Keywords.

   Thus, if someone enters "Seattle plumbing" in search, you will get a 100% match against one of your Keywords, and you may score the full 10 points for Keywords matching.

   If the Keywords are not comma separated, a search for "Seattle plumbing" will deliver a *partial* match, because "Seattle plumbing" is only a *piece* of the Keyword "Seattle plumbing plumbing in Seattle" (note repetition of the word "plumbing"). Such a partial match might score you half of the available 10 points.

   To scoop up your full 10 points, it is important to use commas to separate Keywords.

   Limit your Keywords to seven or fewer. Fewer is better, if fewer covers all the Keywords you want. The more you increase your number of Keywords, the more Google "dilutes" the value of each for that page, so don't squander the value of your most important Keywords by including Keywords that are much less important. Use the other Keyword variations in page content or blog postings on your website. The limit of seven Keywords is *per page*, which is another reason you should separate pages if you think more than seven Keywords are needed.

Text that is longer than about 100,000 characters, including all HTML, is ignored. Break big pages into multiple pages.

4.   **Textual content: 20 points**. The more often Keywords are used in your content, the better score you get.

Keyword density: If "seattle plumbing" appears 10 times out of 10,000 words on a web page, it may get more points than if it appeared 10 times out of 20,000 words on a web page. But remember, stuffing the text with your Keywords can have a negative impact - search engines seem to know when a web page is stuffed.

If your relevant content is growing every day, you scoop up more of these points.

If your content changes significantly every day, Google visits your site more and more frequently. It takes time for it to notice, but it will notice within three of four months if your website is changing every day.

5.   **Latent Semantic Content: 10 points**. Google knows that "chair" and "seat" have a similar meaning. You have probably noticed how when you search for a term, it brings up similar terms in search results. In addition to using the exact Keywords of your choice, use semantically related terms to reinforce Keyword matching. Semantically related terms ("chair" instead of always "seat") reinforce your ownership of the subject. The Google search engine is somehow able to make the association between semantically related words and gives you a better score if it finds them.

6.   **External Keyword reinforcement: 30 points**. The more links you get from sites that "talk about your subject" the more points you get for being associated with those Keywords outside of your own website. Such external Keyword reinforcement is one of the ways in which Inbound Links to your site help you scoop up most of these 30 available points.

Anchor text Inbound links (like this: Life Coaching for Executives) reinforce Keyword ownership better than plain links (like this: www.ici.ie). More on Anchor Text on page 21.

Each page is then given a 'grade' based on its MatchScore:

95-100: A+

90 - 94: A

85 - 89: A-

80 - 84: B+

75 - 79: B

70 - 74: B-

Et cetera.

That first pass is like taking an English exam (at least, like it was in the old days when I used to walk barefoot in the snow to school). You do your best on each of perhaps six questions, which in total offer you a possible 100 points (or percent). Getting full marks on one or two questions, even scoring brilliantly on them, won't give you a pass if you score miserably on all other questions. The points are there for you to get that needed high score. You just have to score well on most if not all questions to score a high grade. And in the end, it's all about getting a high score *relative* to others, not about achieving an *absolute* high score. In other words, a MatchScore of C+ is excellent if competing web pages all score worse than C+. A MatchScore of A- is poor if competing web pages score A+.

Google takes the web pages that score an A+ (for the search words in question) and displays them in the search results, sorted by PageRank; highest to lowest.

You can see just how important Keyword matching is.

- If your page does not match up with the search words, it doesn't matter what PageRank you have.

- In a competitive space, many companies might have worked up an excellent MatchScore, so PageRank becomes the deciding factor for what appears early in search results.

- Keep a religious daily focus on Keyword matching, and keep an eye on your long term PageRank needs - when competition gets hot, you will need that higher PageRank to push your page ahead of others with the same MatchScore.

- Concentrate on individual pages – not your whole website – to score that high MatchScore. Trying to capture a high MatchScore for a large number of search words in a single page is unwise because they dilute the effectiveness of each other. Keep them on separate pages. For example, if you have three very different products, break out each product into a different web page, applying the above rules appropriately to each page.

All you need is a better MatchScore than your competition for those words you really want to own. Very few companies score highly on MatchScore, even for core terms related to their business, because, well, they ignore the basics and make it hard for search engines to give them the scores they might otherwise deserve.

The opportunity is there for companies that know how these simple principles work to excel before their competitors wake up.

Re-visit your older blog entries with new information

Oh, how information fatigues fast!

The "submit" button has hardly cooled when the blog posting you've just made is out of date.

Revisiting old blog postings and updating them with your latest perspective, and with new information, has a two-fold positive effect: (a) the value of the information is potentially increased and (2) search engines see the change as another element of your "rapidly changing content" requirement for Search Engine Optimization.

31.For any of your blog postings, both inside and outside your website, that can be edited after they have been posted, consider rereading them with a view to making corrections, improvements and additions. An updated blog posting is every bit as useful a new addition in the eyes of search engines and tells them that your site is active.

Look at your competitors' Keywords

Most established companies already know what words prospects use to find their product or services on the web. That is, having not yet heard of you at the time they do their search. (When they know who you are, they can search for your company name, but Search Engine Optimization is about connecting with people who've never heard of you).

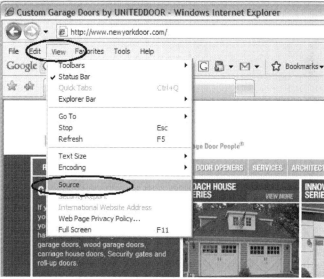

Figure 7 - view page source from Internet Explorer

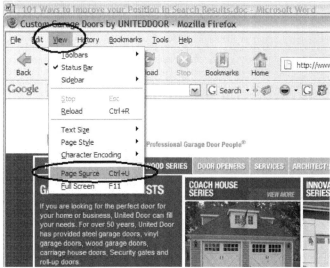

Figure 8 - view page source from Firefox

Figure 9 - sample source code with Keywords highlighted

If you are not so sure what your Keywords should be, you do probably know who your competitors are and you can look at theirs. Look at the home page of any competitor that appears on the first page of Google search results, and view their HTML source. (View/source or View/Page source on the browser menu). With the source window open, search for the word "Keywords" and look at what follows. To examine the source code for any web page, see Figure 7, Figure 8 and Figure 9.

> # 32.View the page source of your successful competitor's home page and look at their Keywords. Cherry-pick from their Keywords to supplement your own.

Focusing on *high quality* Inbound Links

You can find the raw number of Inbound Links to your website by typing in "links: www.mywebsite.com" (where "mywebsite" is your website) into Google search. The raw count of links to your website is one indicator of how your SEO efforts are progressing, but remember that the *quality* of each inbound link has an enormous influence on its effect.

A link from the home page of IBM, with its PageRank of 9 and probably a very high TrustRank, might represent enough Inbound Links to to build your entire business on the web, if you are a small company.

One high quality link can be worth several hundred mediocre quality links.

Still, everything adds up. Links of lesser value might not be as important from a PageRank point of view, but some such "lower value" Inbound Links can offer a different reward: they might drive visitors to your website because people click them.

Inbound links have three possible functions (1) increasing your PageRank, (2) driving visitors to your site via click-through, and (3) educating people about your existence when they see the link, even if they do not click it.

In addition, if the site containing the link has content closely related to the content on your website, your "ownership of the subject" is further reinforced, particularly if the link contains relevant Anchor Text. (See page 21 for a description of Anchor Text.)

33.When you are making a posting to a website with a view to making an Inbound Link from it back to your website, take note of the website's PageRank[2]. A link from a website with a higher PageRank is worth more than a link from a website with a lower PageRank. Choose the former over the latter.

Write and submit articles to article directories

How long has it been since you wrote a school essay? How long would it take you to write one today on your current area of expertise?

There are places on the web that accept and publish articles on a wide variety of topics.

34.Take a look at Ezine Articles (see link below) for ideas on how you might write and submit your own article. In some cases, articles are picked up by other sites and published elsewhere, taking the embedded links back to your website with them.

http://www.ezinearticles.com/

---

[2] To find the Google PageRank of a page, visit www.prchecker.info

To every Marketing Executive: Save Nothing for the Swim Back

The Internet's "New World Order" forces you into total commitment to a web strategy. To survive, your business must appear on Page One of search results when people search for what you offer.

80% of success is just showing up
— **Woody Allen**

How prescient Woody Allen was when he said it! I doubt he's interested in SEO, but what he said applies well to Search Engine Optimization. If you have a business that doesn't "show up" early in search results, you may be missing the bulk of sales opportunities.

...nor the battle to the strong

In the 1997 science fiction movie Gattaca, a Utopian age of "designer babies" set in the future lets parents control their child's characteristics by cherry-picking from their own genes. What's more, ones place in society is determined by this government-registered gene profile selected by ones parents. A subplot of the movie is - and some would argue its main plot - two brothers play out their sibling rivalry, with the officially inferior one, Vincent Freeman (played by Ethan Hawke) always outwitting his supposedly superior brother, Anton Freeman (played by Loren Dean). Towards the end of the movie, the weaker brother explains why he always wins, despite his brother's government-verified superior genes. Vincent says he wins because he, unlike his brother, "never saves anything for the swim back".

The race is not to the swift, nor the battle to the strong, neither yet bread to the wise, nor yet riches to men of understanding, nor yet favour to men of skill; but time and chance happeneth to them all.
— **- Ecclesiastes**

As a marketing professional, you often wonder why you're not delivering the quantity and quality of leads you ought to. Where do prospects live, congregate and search for products or services like yours, you ask yourself. Is it the recession? Global warming, perhaps? Where are they, for crying out loud!

Less and less do prospects rely on trade shows, conferences and brochures to find sales leads. More and more do they use the web to find them.

> ***Any noun can be verbed***
> **– Dan Davis**

You know you're in business when your co. name is a verb.

Google first broke ground in 1998 and within several years their company name became a verb. You know you're in business when your company name becomes a verb. (I've never heard someone say "I Microsofted it" - although let's be polite and not guess what it might mean if they did). The verb "Google" is so ubiquitous today that actors use the term in TV shows. Old people (like me) say "I searched the Internet for it". Young people say "I Google'd it". Google became a verb so quickly, spell checkers don't yet recognize the word "Google".

Look at the business you are in today. Perhaps there are dozens or maybe even a hundred or so businesses competing at least a little with your business. Now consider this: unless you are in a tech-savvy, Internet-savvy line of business, only a small percentage of that hundred or so have woken up to the real power of finding business on the web. Is your company in that small percentage, or are you one of the sleepers? Do you even know on which page of search results your website appears today?

Only a small percentage of businesses have woken up to the "New World Order" of the Internet.

Possession is nine tenths of the law

It is easier to "maintain ownership of the hilltop" than it is to get there, and when your business appears on page one of search results you are on that hilltop. If no one in your space has their act together yet, it will cost you a lot less to take that hilltop today. And once you command that hilltop, it will be an order of magnitude more difficult (and more expensive) for a competitor to displace you (or you them, if they beat you to it!). When your website is on the first page of search results, you are generating more profit and using some of that profit to help you stay on Page One, the hilltop.

40% of business-to-consumer commerce is secured via the web. Over 80% of business-to-business commerce is secured that way. Both percentages continue to increase and there's no going back to the old way of finding new customers. You need to commit to your web strategy before your competitor does to theirs.

The question is, are you prepared to save nothing for the swim back? Perhaps you are a very smart marketing professional. Perhaps you are the smarter sibling in that Gattaca movie. Unfortunately, however, everything you learned about marketing in college you can flush down the toilet. The question now is, are you confident enough to let all of that go, and bold enough to save nothing for the swim back?

Almost all search is local

When people use search engines to find something, they often include a city or town name in the search words. For example, "life coach seattle" instead of "life coach", or "car glass seattle" and not "car glass". In addition, search engines use the computer address of the person doing the search to determine the general location of their computer and tailor the search to match it.

If your product or service tends to be confined to where you are located, make sure your city or town name is included in your home page's Title Tag. In other words, if you own a pet grooming business in Albany, New York, your market is local, and your websites should contain references to your location. Conversely, if you sell hand-made dolls online, the city your business location is not important.

> # 35.If your target customers are in a specific area, use the names of those areas in the target pages relating to those areas.

Keep an eye on your PageRank

PageRank is a log scale, not a linear scale

If it were a linear scale, a PageRank of 5 would be simply 25% more valuable than a PageRank of 4, but in reality, a PageRank of 5 is approximately 5x the value of a PageRank of 4. So too is a PageRank of 8 about 5x the value of a PageRank of 7.

Google sets the value of all these PageRanks, and the exact formula is a well-guarded secret. In addition, they refine and modify the formula regularly. They store the calculated PageRanks of all indexed pages on the web in one of their databases.

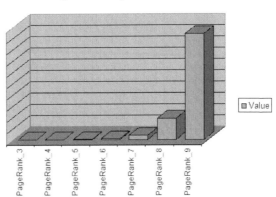

PageRank and PageRank Value

Figure 10 - PageRank and relative value

Let's say your PageRank was 3. As you look at the New York Times home page, with a PageRank of 9, you could be forgiven for thinking its PageRank was 3 times the value of your PageRank. In actuality, the NY Times home page PageRank is worth tens of thousands of times the value of your PageRank.

A PageRank of 5 is actually "five-point something", not necessarily 5.00; it could be 5.04 or 5.98. I don't know how many decimal places Google holds for every PageRank it stores, but one or two decimal places would hold enough significance - 5.22 or 5.2 is as meaningful as 5.22363292 - the number is an approximation to begin with.

36.Take a note of the PageRank of your Home Page at the same time every week. Populate a spreadsheet with the value and track it over time. Take note of your top competitors' PageRanks. A Chart based on the data, especially if your efforts push your PageRank ahead of your competitors', makes a compelling report to attach to your annual performance review!

Keywords metatag

For a given page, the number of Keywords dilutes the effectiveness of each Keyword.

Almost every website you visit has too many Keywords stuffed into the Keyword metatag. Although Keywords are not as significant as they used to be in the eyes of search engines, they do contribute to your overall success in search engine placement. Let's look at an example of Keywords done well and one done poorly.

```
Source of: http://www.newyorkdoor.com/ - Mozilla Firefox
File  Edit  View  Help
<!DOCTYPE HTML PUBLIC "-//W3C//DTD HTML 4.01 Frameset//EN"
   "http://www.w3.org/TR/html4/frameset.dtd">
<html>
<head>
<title>Custom Garage Doors by UNITEDDOOR</title>
<meta name="keywords" content="Wood garage doors, carriage house door, coach
house door, custom wood door, garage door, garage door opener">
<meta name="generator" content="Misk.com Domain Cloaking 2">
</head>
<frameset rows="100%,*" cols="100%" framespacing="0" frameborder="no"
border="0">
   <frame name="Misk" scrolling="auto" src="http://www.uniteddoor.com"
noresize>
   <noframes>
   Please go to: <a
href="http://www.uniteddoor.com">http://www.uniteddoor.com</a>
   </noframes>
</frameset>
</html>
Line 12, Col 37
```

Figure 11 - example of Keywords done well

I just plucked this website off the top of my head. No surprise, the website existed: www.newyorkdoor.com. If you look at the source for the page that opens (menu bar View/Page Source in Firefox or View/Source in Internet Explorer) you will see that they have just 6 Keywords. Note that the term "Keyword" can refer to more than one word.

Keywords must be separated by commas.

When there are too many Keywords, the effectiveness of each Keyword is weakened, or "diluted".

The image in Figure 12 is from a website that has too many Keywords. The more Keywords within the Keyword metatag of a single web page, the less effective each one is. This makes sense of course, as search engines try to create the best match for the search words that a person browsing the web uses; if you had, for example, only one Keyword, it is more likely that is exactly what your web page is all about.

```
<!DOCTYPE HTML PUBLIC "-//W3C//DTD HTML 4.01 Transitional//EN"
"http://www.w3.org/TR/html4/loose.dtd">
<html>
<head>
<meta name="robots" content="index, follow"><meta name="description" content="All natural
skincare for dogs instantly relieves itching & redness. Treats mange, dermatitis, hot spots and
all skin conditions! GUARANTEED:"><meta name="keywords" content="all natural dog,dog skin,dog
organic skin care,dog infection,canine dermatitis,Dog Dry Skin ,Dog dermatitis,Dog Hot Spot,Cat
Hot Spot,Itchy Skin Dogs,dog skin disease,Fur Regrowth,dog dermatitis,Dog Mange,dog
allergy,mange treatment,mange,dog mange,cat mange"><META HTTP-EQUIV="CACHE-CONTROL"
CONTENT="NO-CACHE"><META HTTP-EQUIV="PRAGMA" CONTENT="NO-CACHE">
<script language="javascript">
//-- These colors are used in design templates

var col_primary="";
var col_secondary="";
var col_tertiary="#343c60";
```

Figure 12 - example of Keywords done poorly

In the web page illustrated in Figure 13, no Keywords exist, throwing away a free way to help search engines make a Keyword match with their website.

Some websites have omitted Keywords completely, and others forget to place a comma between Keywords. If commas are left out, all the Keywords are essentially considered to be a single Keyword, which would make it all but impossible for a search engine to make an exact match.

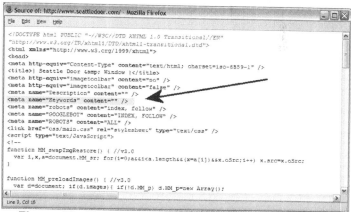

Figure 13 - Example of page with missing Keywords

37.For each significant page on your website – your home page, for instance – view the source (from the menu bar). Search the text for the text "Keywords" (including the quotes) and make sure the correct Keywords for that page are there.

Contacting the author

I want you to be satisfied with this book. If you have a question about any part of it, please post it at the following unpublished location, and include your email address if you would like me to contact you directly.

www.foreverup.com/bm/magnet

You can view others' comments and questions and keep up-to-date with any new developments in Search Engine Optimization that I have learned of after the book went to press.

My guarantee to you

If you didn't get what you expected from this book, return the book within 30 days of purchase, in any condition to:
Liam Scanlan
12819 SE 38th St. #146
Bellevue WA 98006, USA
I will send you a check for $12.
Please include a copy of your purchase receipt, and include your mailing address so I can send the refund to you.

The closer to the top, the greater % convert to sales

Getting paid twice

When people searching for the product or service you offer find you higher up on search results, they are more likely to buy from you. So, not only do more people see your business, but a *greater percentage of those* are likely to buy from you!

Researchers have found that the actual % of closed business from leads generated on Page One is higher.

For example, for every 1,000 leads generated on Page One, you might convert 1.3% to sales, and for every 1,000 leads generated from page seven, you might generate 1.0% to sales.

This means not only that you get more visitors when you appear on the first page of search results, but your company gains more credibility for appearing there.

A mere 15% of people using Google Search look beyond the first two pages of search results.

85% of business-to-business shoppers begin the transaction on the web.

About 40% of consumers do their shopping on the web.

With numbers like those, any company that wants to sell its product or service needs to be in the first page or two of Google search results.

Supporting statistics can be seen on MarketingSherpa's website.

38.Define your target daily visitor count.
Install Google Analytics into your website. Take note of the number of visitors that arrive at your site using search. The majority of them should arrive through search. If, for example, 20% of them arrived like that, there is a huge opportunity to expand that percentage.
Let's say 50 unique visitors arrived through search and 200 arrived by other means every day. If your site were optimized for search engines, you could reasonably expect 40 – 80% from search, and that number would be between 160 and 800, not a paltry 50. So, your overall visitor count would be between 360 and 1,000, up from 250.

Making it easy for others to add links to your page

Your website should have several methods of passing the good word on.

A quick way to allow your readers to pass the word on to others is by installing a component called AddThis, available free from www.addthis.com, to your website. Rather than try to add each online community (MySpace, FaceBook, etc.) separately, this little nugget gives users the option to pick from many different ways of adding a link to your website. Take a look at the AddThis website and click the Add This button that you see close to the top of the page.

This is a more passive method (passive for you, because you don't have to do anything - you let your website visitors decide when and where an Inbound Link is created) than going out to add Inbound Links yourself.

39.Visit the site www.addthis.com and install their free widget into your website on every page. This will enable visitors to add your website to their communities (like MySpace, FaceBook, etc.).

Managing Title Tag for every web page

The importance of Page Title to search results

The first order of business in getting your page to appear early in search results is matching the words on your website with the search words that people use to find products or services like yours. And probably the most important text on your web page is that which appears on the top of the browser when you are viewing that page. That text comes from a specific place in the HTML of the web page; it is called the Title Tag.

Let's look at an example:

Enter the words "strategies international" into Google search. As it turns out, "Strategies International" is the first two words in the page title of the website www.strategiesintl.com. Strategies International's website appears as the 6th item on page 1 of search results, even with a PageRank of zero. That's how powerful Page Title is to search engines. (By the way: A PageRank of zero is actually zero-point-something - Google does not say what the actual number is - just the rounded down integer).

To give you an idea of just how simple this is, the following line is the fourth line of HTML in Strategies International's home page:

<title>Strategies International</title>

The Title Tag is perhaps the most significant influence on Keyword matching in search results.

This illustrates the importance of placing your very best Keywords in first position of the title tag of the web page that you want to appear higher on search results. Yes, your PageRank plays a role too, as do a number of other factors, but title tag on the page is the most important Keyword location as far as search engines are concerned. Another very important source of Keywords is the domain name. The effect of title tag, domain name, Keywords and content are covered in detail, beginning on page 45.

40. Examine the title tag on each important page of your website. To do that, open each in a browser and look at the text in the very top bar of your browser. That text comes from the text between <title> and </title> illustrated in Figure 14.

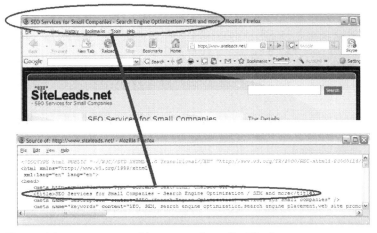

Figure 14 - every page title comes from its title tag

You know 400 things about your business

Many people tell me they have no idea what to put in their blog. I tell them to think about their business in terms of all the little nuggets of wisdom they picked up over the years they have been in that line of business.

Let's say you were a Life Coach. Think of the little assertions you've made to your clients over the years. See the list below - I got it off the top of the head of my Life Coach brother. A Life Coach would be able to write a paragraph to match each header. Make your own list of such topics/points. Each header + paragraph will become a single day's blog entry. Start your list as soon as you can and over the course of several months you should be able to come up with about 400. Here's the first four: (not for your business of course, but for a one-person life coaching business)

1. Clarify what you want from life today

2. How to raise your self-awareness

3. Developing your emotional self-mastery

4. Building quality relationships

Each of the four topics would be followed by a paragraph or two.

Over the course of a year, you will have built a treasure trove of value for people visiting your website. That will drive traffic and keep people coming back again and again. It will increase visitor counts to your website, and bring you more and more business. That is how the Internet works today. I know, it takes a bit of faith to do all that content work up-front.

The other significant part of the equation is Inbound Link creation.

41.Every business person I know has nuggets of wisdom they have collected over the years. Start writing yours down in a little notepad or in your computer. Each nugget will form the basis of a posting to the blog in your website. You don't need to think of all 400 today. Start with a dozen; build from there.

Effect of "nofollow" tag on value of Inbound Links

The "nofollow" tag asks search engines to ignore a given link for the purposes of increasing the PageRank of the page it points to. It should really be called the "nocount" or "novote" tag if you were to ask me.

If your objective is to increase your PageRank by creating Inbound Links to your site, don't spend too much time creating posts to sites that use the *nofollow* tag.

How do you know if an Inbound Link will be counted?

Open an existing posting on the site in question. Click View Source (View/Source menu in Internet Explorer, or View/Page Source in Firefox). Search for the term "nofollow" in the source. If you find it close to where the person who made the posting placed his/her link, chances are, links coming from that site will have the nofollow tag and will not count towards your own PageRank either.

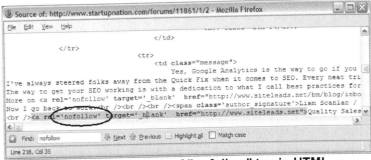

Figure 15 - example of "nofollow" tag in HTML

42.When you find a place on the web to which you can post an entry to point back to your website, once you have made the first posting, examine the HTML source code where your link is and take note of whether or not the <nofollow> tag is present. If it is, consider that a potentially "low quality" Inbound Link.
Give more attention to websites where the <nofollow> tag is not present.

Keep Keywords to a minimum

The Keyword tag in any page is best served by limiting the number of words to as few as possible. It is hard to say exactly at what threshold the search engines begin to "dilute" the effectiveness of Keywords. It might be 10 or 5, or 7. If 3 is all you really need, limit it to 3.

> **# 43.Keep Keyword count on *each web page* to seven or fewer.**

There is a temptation to insert dozens of words (see example in Figure 16) into the Keyword tag section of your web page, and there might be pages out there that truly need to do that, but most web pages do not have such a broad reach. Use the body text of the page to contain all the words you are interested in supporting or split a page into multiple pages and make each a unique "SEO Target Page" in its own right.

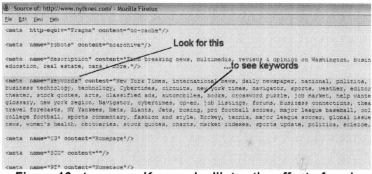

Figure 16 - too many Keywords dilutes the effect of each

> **# 44.If you must hold on to all your Keywords, split pages into multiple pages until each has seven or fewer.**

"Gaming" the search engines

When good websites do bad things

Google, and indeed other search engines, decide what gets displayed in search results based on Best Value to the Customer.

The better the search results for the person doing the search, the more competitive a given engine's search offering is, and the more customers return again and again to find what they need.

When someone does a search, Google wants the very best result to appear. What displays is the result of many automated processes on lots of metadata ("data about data") relating to web pages on the Internet. With so much at stake, many companies and people come up with elaborate mechanisms or "tricks" to fool search engines into overrating a particular web page or website. As the last decade advanced (it's 2008 as I write this), search engine companies got smarter and smarter about outmaneuvering such tricksters. Such tricky behavior is called "Black Hat". Good behavior is called "White Hat".

Black Hat versus White Hat

Activities that try to "trick" search engines are called "Black Hat". Activities that add value to the customer's experience in a genuine, honest way are known as "White Hat".

> # 45.Avoid embedding links to your web page into objects that sit on other people's websites.

No matter what idea you come up with for improving your position in search engine results, ask yourself this question: *Does what I am doing add value to the visitor on the web?* If the answer is No, then avoid it. If the link does provide value to the person viewing the page, consider including it.

> # 46.Be suspicious of any activity that claims it will lift your position in search results quickly. Look for content-related activities that add value to the reader's experience.

If a webmaster engages in enough so-called Black Hat activity, their website stands the risk of being penalized by search engines.

That is, losing some or all of their PageRank or being blacklisted altogether.

47.Avoid reciprocal links just for the sake of increasing a website's Inbound Link count.

Even if you are a non-technical person, you can always ask the question *Does what I am doing add value to the visitor on the web?*

48.Avoid (a) white text on a white background making search engines think you are hiding text from the reader, but trying to hook the search engines with it, (b) automating the regular stuffing of text into your website to make the search engines think you have "rapidly changing content" and (c) anything that automates the process of inbound link generation.

Best ways to create Inbound Links to your website

Selecting the best pages to link to

49.Pick a small number of pages on your website for long term targeting with Inbound Links. Two or three is typical for a small company with limited funds for Internet marketing.

If you work for a large company, with lots of products and services, you could have a large number of Target Pages.

Google's thumbnail judgment of a website is termed *PageRank* and not *WebsiteRank* because Google gives a rank to every *page*, not to every website. Yes, there is a connection between pages on a website – pages within a website have an effect on each other's

PageRank – but there are many examples of widely varying PageRanks across pages on the very same website.

> # 50.To minimize Bounce Rate[3], when you create Inbound Links, target the highest value web pages on your website. This makes it more likely visitors will continue viewing your website after reading the page they arrived at.

For example: Your website has twelve pages, but you want to drive traffic to two of the twelve pages in particular: the Products page and the Services page. You might also consider the homepage itself, but whichever pages you select for SEO targeting, make sure they are the best candidates for eventual arrival of visitors when they click a link somewhere on the web and come to your website. The "best experience first" principle is why real estate executives show the best room of the house first if they can.

When selecting pages on your website for SEO targeting: (i.e., the pages of your website that you want visitors to arrive on from other websites):

1. Keep it to a small number of pages (e.g. "http://www.justcauseit.com/channels/education" and "http://www.justcauseit.com/channels/arts")

2. If in doubt, use your homepage (e.g. http://www.justcauseit.com)

3. Expect the target pages to exist long into the future. Don't pick pages you know will be gone from your website soon, so that when people do click the link to your site, make sure they land on a page with high quality content that you expect to be around for a long time.

---

[3] Bounce Rate means the % of visitors that follow a link to your website and leave before viewing any other page on your website

51. If you MUST delete a page that has Inbound Links pointing to it, replace the exact page – making sure the URL remains unchanged – with a page containing a link to the new page or to your homepage (this will prevent the message "Error 404" from appearing when a visitor follows the link to your website).

If you want to find out how many links there are to a specific page, go to Google Search and type: (replace the URL with yours) **links: justcauseit.com/channels/arts**

Finding Inbound Link opportunities

Central to making quality Inbound Links is your knowledge of your own business.

52. Take a nugget of wisdom relating to your business and offer it to the world via a forum, blog or bulletin board on the web that talks about that subject, and link that contribution back to one of the SEO Target Pages on your own web page. Try to do this at least once per week.

It sounds easy, but it can be challenging.

What is the most important aspect of where a link is coming from? Its location, so a link from a page on ibm.com, assuming it is one with a high PageRank, will be worth a lot more than a link from mcSchmuckLumber.com. Here are the things you want to consider when finding opportunities for, and creating an Inbound Links from, external websites:

1.   High traffic sites

2.   Pages with higher PageRanks than yours.

3.   Locations relevant to your business (if you are in the clothing business, a link from a lumber site is less valuable, unless it is about, for example, clothing for lumber workers).

53.Instead of listing your raw URL (e.g. http://www.ici.ie), use Anchor Text (International Coaching Institute) with the link behind it. That tells the search engines a lot about the content on the website the link is pointing to, and come search time, raises your MatchScore because Inbound Links to your web page reinforce your ownership of the subject.

Offer valuable information to a forum, blog, bulletin board or other active community dealing in your subject earning you the right to add the link back to your site. The link rewards you in two ways (1) it increases your raw Inbound Link count determined by search engines and (2) it offers visitors the chance to click the link and come to your site. That second reward is more effective when they like what they read in the posting you made, and they see a direct connection to the subject when they come to your site.

Avoid Cloaking

What is "Cloaking" and how does it affect search results?

Cloaking is a Black Hat method (for a description of what Black Hat means, see page 70) of providing the search engines with one type of page and the visitor/reader with a different page.

Search engines have largely wised up to "cloaking". In any case it is bad business practice. Best practices for the web mean delivering value to your customers and prospects every day. From that perspective, tricking them with false search results is definitely not good business, even if you could get away with it.

54.Beware of services that offer automated Inbound Link creation by embedding your web page address into a widget that is given away for "free" to unsuspecting website owners whose websites have no connection with your business. Such services are attempting to artificially inflate the number of links to your website, but are considered to be Black Hat activities that could cause your website to be blacklisted.

Get all influences working - then the lights go on.

I remember when I was a child; my family one year had a set of Christmas tree lights that operated in series. When one bulb blew out, the whole set of lights went off. The electricity had to pass through each bulb before it went to the next bulb, like links in a chain. The operation of replacing a blown bulb was understandably challenging. You had to remove each bulb, replace it with a good one, and then put back the original if it still didn't work. So, with a 100-bulb set, you might spend 10 minutes just working out which bulb had failed.

SEO (Search Engine Optimization) is a bit like a set of in-series Christmas tree lights. You have to have all (or at least many) the bulbs working before the lights go on. For competitive spaces in the market – where companies are dedicated to SEO – you need many of these factors working in your favor, but for less competitive spaces, all you need is to nudge ahead of your competitors who might not be paying any attention.

Let's focus on one of the biggest factors, and see how it depends on other factors. Inbound Links.

Inbound links play a huge role in keeping your PageRank in shape. Why? Because if people find your information interesting, they are more likely to create a link to it from their own blog, MySpace, FaceBook or whichever online community they frequent on the Internet. Thus, search engines look favorably upon a growing and sizable list of Inbound Links. In the eyes of search engines, Inbound Links = Interest = Value.

Organic Inbound Link growth (Inbound Links that visitors create to your website) is dependent upon traffic. The problem is, how do people find your website in the first place, in order to create an inbound link to it?

> # 55.Be patient. A website that is only four months old can't expect to have a high PageRank. Keep adding to your blog, and adding Inbound Links to it. It will reach critical mass eventually. Add Inbound Links at every opportunity.

Organic Inbound Link growth

Organic Inbound Link growth is when visitors are regularly adding Inbound Links to your website. Organic Inbound Link growth is totally dependent upon traffic. If only you had the traffic to build the Inbound Links to build the traffic! It's a bit of a Catch 22 situation.

There are two things you have to do to get the Inbound Links growing on their own:

1. Manually create the first wave of Inbound Links. Expect to create several new links every week for about 6 months.

2. Make it extremely easy for people to bookmark / tag your web page. (See following Action Item).

For as long as you want more traffic to your website, manually creating Inbound Links is what you must engage in regularly.

Make it extremely easy: I recommend using an add-in like the one available on the AddThis website to make it easy for your website visitors to bookmark your site. All you have to do is add a few lines of HTML (supplied by AddThis) to any web page you'd like to have this feature on, and the rest is up to visitors. In addition, the AddThis website reports on how many folks use it and where they link from.

> # 56.Visit www.addthis.com. Use their free html and add it to your website. It will help others add a link to your website.

As long as you want more traffic to your website, manually creating Inbound Links is what you must engage in several times a week.

Inbound Links often take weeks to be picked up by search engines. My rule-of-thumb is four to six weeks before the effect of

Inbound Links can be measured. But don't be disheartened - keep creating new ones - and remember to make every posting on the web interesting, useful, succinct and accurate.

The effect of PageRank on search results position [Part 1]

There is a lot of controversy surrounding the role PageRank plays in where a page displays in Google search results. Some say it has a big effect; others say it is largely unimportant, so I ran some tests.

Using the search words "investment services", I noted the PageRank of every web page listed on each of the first 10 pages of search results. I then averaged out the numbers per search results page. I added up all PageRanks of the ten pages of the first page of search results and divided the result by ten (to get the average). I repeated the process for the other 9 pages of search results and charted the results. See Figure 17.

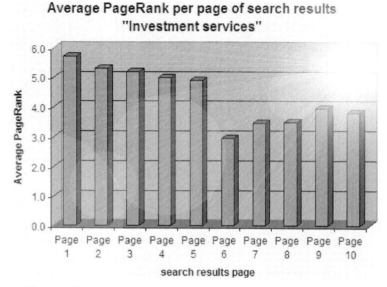

Figure 17 - average PageRanks for "investment services"

Looking at Figure 17, the pattern is clear; the better a page's PageRank, the greater chance it has of appearing earlier in search results. There are lots of other factors of course but PageRank clearly plays a role.

Some interesting things about the results:

1.   How quickly the average PageRank goes from "5-point-something" to "3-point something"! With the thousands upon thousands of investment services companies across the web, only a few dozen have secured a good enough PageRank to get into the first few pages of search results. In less technical markets, PageRanks drop off significantly after only a half dozen pages of search results. The first ten pages were the first in about 32 million pages that matched the search words. (There are billions of pages on the Internet).

The second interesting thing is, I would have thought Investment Services companies would have the resources to get their web presence competitive, their PageRank up, and their Keywords optimized in order to appear early in search results. There seems to be little effort to do so, suggesting a big opportunity for the company that focuses on it.

57. If you are in a less competitive business space, where the PageRanks of the web pages on the first page of search results are low (less than 4), you have an opportunity to move to the top of search results in a few months. Keep an eye on the PageRank of your home page Use www.prchecker.info to find your PageRank). Take a note of your PageRank on the same day every week, as well as the page number of search results you appear on for a given set of search words. Use the same search words every week.

All else being equal, higher PageRank'd pages go to the top of search results.

Thus, there is a huge opportunity for lesser companies to steal the show and get ahead of bigger players in search results.

The effect of PageRank on search results position [Part 2]

In the previous section, I illustrated the effect of PageRank using a single search example. The first ten pages of search results were examined to see if there was a noticeable trend in PageRanks as we looked at each set of web pages, and their respective PageRanks, all the way from search results page 1 to search results page 10; about 100 web pages in all. The trend looked pretty obvious; Higher PageRanks tended to appear earlier in search results.

The second example was with the search term "psychiatric services" and it came up with a very similar pattern to the previous experiment with the search words "investment services".   See Figure 18.

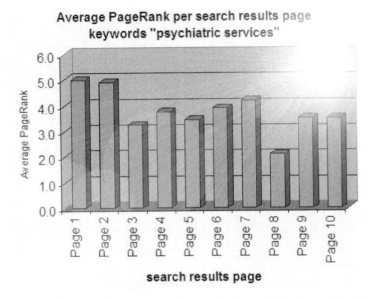

Figure 18 - results for search words "psychiatric services"

Although the average PageRanks for the 2nd experiment were lower across the board that experiment #1, the trend was the same. Pages with higher PageRanks tended towards the top of search results.

Note: to get the average PageRank for all ten pages on a single search results page, I added .5 to each result, except where there was "no PageRank". I added the .5 because Google shows only integer value of the PageRank. For example, PageRank of 4 can be any floating point value between 4 and 5 (e.g. 4.7130826). Thus, "4.5" is statistically more likely to be nearer the actual PageRank value of "4", than 4.00 is. For PageRanks that are "not available" I assumed a PageRank of zero.

I then did the same experiment on a poorly served (in terms of technology) industry: Pawnbrokers (see Figure 19). Although PageRank values were very low across the board, the same basic pattern is discernible.

In addition, there is clearly an opportunity where PageRanks are low. A PageRank of 4 is not that hard to achieve; in the pawnbroker example, a modest effort would put a website right to the top of search results.

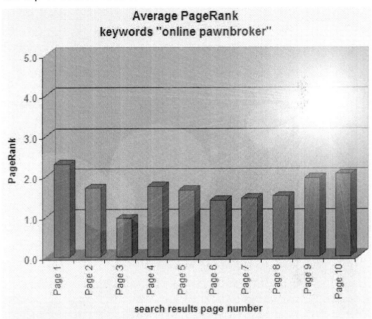

Figure 19 - results for search words "online pawnbroker"

Conclusions:

1.   A higher PageRank increases your chances of appearing closer to the top of search results.

2.   Page One of search results almost always has a higher average PageRank than any other search results page.

3.   Roughly speaking, Keyword matching is done first, and then within each level of Keyword matching, PageRank is the next sort order.

4.   If a page has excellent Keyword matching (MatchScore), it will appear ahead of less well matched pages with higher PageRanks.

5.   Setting up your page for matching search words with page content is the First Priority of Search Engine Optimization (SEO).

6.   Maintaining a competitive PageRank is the Second Priority of the SEO executive.

7.   The more competitive the industry (i.e. the more money in it) the sharper the trend line in PageRanks across the first 10 pages of search results.

The effect of PageRank on search results position [Part 3]

One more test.

A PageRank of 4 or 5 will be enough for this Designer Handbag company to reach Page One of search results at least for some important Keywords.

Boen and Gill in Seattle wanted to understand how much of a challenge it would be to get their website to the top of search results. I ran the same test using the search term "designer handbags" as I had done earlier (previous topics). I wanted to see what they were up against in terms of established companies on the web.

As expected, Boen and Gill's home page, with a PageRank of 2, did not appear in the first ten pages. The web pages 1 through 10 listed on the first page of Google search results had the following respective PageRanks: (see Figure 20)

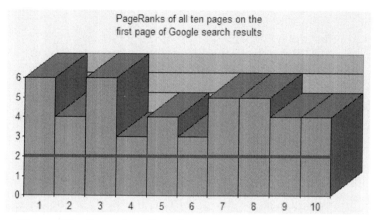

Figure 20 - Page One PageRanks for "designer handbags"

Not surprisingly, with the big money industry of high fashion at stake, there appears to be some serious competition for the first page of Google search results. For the results of this particular search, the average PageRank on the first page was 4.9, an almost full point above the average of the second page (which was also the 2nd highest average of all ten pages) of search results, which was 4.1.

Still, for Boen and Gill to ascend sufficiently from PageRank 2 (illustrated by the black horizontal line in the chart above) is not impossible by any means; there are even a couple of PageRank 3 pages on the first page of results. (For those PageRank 3s that reached page one of search results, Keyword matching scores – MatchScore – would have been high). With a concerted effort toward ideal Keyword matches, a PageRank of 4 or 5 will be enough for Boen and Gill to reach the first page of search results at least for some important searches.

The question is – as it is for every such company – does Boen and Gill want to invest the effort in getting PageRank, Keyword Density and Frequency of changing content in order to appear on Page One of search results in the five or so months' timeframe it will take to get there?

58.You can't manage what you can't measure.
Make note today of the PageRank of your home page.
Measure it against the PageRanks of all ten web pages on
the first page of search results. Draw a line where your
current PageRank is in relation to those ten, just like the
chart in Figure 20. This will give you an instant feel for how
far away arrival on Page One is for your website.

What is the dollar value of a PageRank?

Here is an estimation of the dollar values of PageRanks 0 to 9. I
deliberately left out PageRank 10 because I only know of a single
company that has it, and that is Google. No surprise there.

Google PageRanks estimated dollar values:

PageRank	Low	High
PageRank 0	$100	$2,500
PageRank 1	500	5,000
PageRank 2	1,000	10,000
PageRank 3	3,000	15,000
PageRank 4	10,000	75,000
PageRank 5	25,000	200,000
PageRank 6	125,000	750,000
PageRank 7	500,000	6,000,000
PageRank 8	5,000,000	50,000,000
PageRank 9	10,000,000	250,000,000

As you can see, the lower PageRanks are not of much value to an
established company. Even a single-person company needs to be

aiming for a PageRank of 4 or more. For us at SiteLeads.net, we are aiming to have a PageRank of 5 by about April 2009.

A high PageRank is ineffective if the page it refers to does not have the right Keywords. The Right Keywords + Best PageRank = Success.

The relative value of a website, and the cost of increasing PageRank, increases exponentially.

A PageRank of 5 can be achieved through the diligent efforts of a single person.

A PageRank of 6 takes a small marketing team.

A PageRank of 7 can happen when the focused resources of a well-established company are applied.

A PageRank of 8 requires a large, well-established company dedicated to its web presence.

PageRanks are displayed as their integer value only, although they are stored as a floating point number. For example, PageRank 5 is actually "five point something" -- It could be 5.124383; it could be 5.98188427 -- reflecting a wide range of possible values.

PageRank 9 is where the truly big, high tech companies like Apple, Microsoft and IBM live.

There is a difference between "no PageRank" and a PageRank of zero. PageRank 0 is "zero point something". "No PageRank" is zero.

Keyword Density and crisp posts

Keep your posts relevant, unambiguous and brief.

Relevant:

The message you are trying to convey should always be relevant to the subject of your blog. For example, if your blog is about deep sea fishing, don't blog about your big office move or your favorite automobile; blog about deep sea fishing.

Unambiguous:

Remove any doubt about the point you are making, and use the precise word for the occasion. Give an example and a screenshot with callouts to illustrate your point if that helps the reader understand the point you are making.

Brief:

Don't ramble on. Don't repeat yourself, unless as a point of clarification.

Take a look at the blog entry in illustrated below. It is a classic example of small talk. It weakens ownership of the subject on the website because it discusses a topic (the office move) that is irrelevant to the subject of the website blog (University admissions).

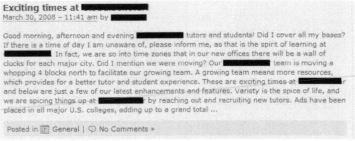

Figure 21 – example of a rambling post

Inbound Links vary a lot in quality

Inbound Links are links on the Internet that people can click which will bring them directly to your website.

Many of us interested in improving our place in search results look for opportunities to create what are called Inbound Links to a page or pages on our website (or websites). That is because we know Google, MSN, Yahoo! and other search engines count the number of these Inbound Links; the more you have, the "more important" you are, and the more priority you get.

Not all Inbound Links are equal.

There are three rough groupings that reflect relative value of Inbound Links.

Basic Link

This is when a page on your website is referenced from somewhere on the Internet simply as the exact URL. For example http://www.ici.ie/index.php. Let us say for comparison purposes this kind of link is worth $100.

Anchor Text Link

Anchor text is where the URL is not immediately visible to the reader, but English words (or other spoken language) are displayed, and the web link is "hidden" behind the English words; all you see is blue underlined text. For example: "You might be interested in one-on-one executive coaching to help you be more successful in business". The underlined text hints at a possible link. This link might be worth several times what a basic link is worth.

> # 59.Always use Anchor Text instead of a raw link wherever you can, using words that are directly related to the subject on the page being linked to.

High Source Value Anchor Text Link

This is like #2 above, but the link is coming from a web page of "high importance". For example, a link from a website of a higher PageRank than yours is worth more than a basic link or an anchor text link. For example, an anchor text link from the American Medical Association's website, which as I write this has a PageRank of 7, pointing to one of your web pages, would be worth a lot, especially if there were very few links going out from that page.

On our imaginary dollar scale, such a link might be worth $1,000 or more.

An Anchor Text link is worth more than a Basic link because the words in the anchored text give search engines clues about what the subject is and consequently reinforce subject ownership for the Anchor Text words. When you create Inbound Links, whenever possible make it an Anchor Text link, paying special attention to the words you use in the Anchor Text. You don't always have control over what the anchor text is, because it is usually someone else's website you're adding to, but if you do, choose words that likely *reinforce the subject on the page it links to.*

60. Although they are generally harder to secure, try to get links to your website from web pages that have a high PageRank. They can be worth several orders of magnitude more than links from unimportant websites.

We have a PageRank of 4. Is that good enough?

The short answer is: It depends.

If your competitors' PageRanks are in the 5s and 6s or above, then no; your PageRank of 4 isn't high enough. If you competitors' PageRanks are in the 2s and 3s, you're in good shape, at least in terms of PageRank.

The real question to ask is "We have a PageRank that is above our competitors' PageRanks. Is that good enough?"

The answer is yes, probably. I say *probably* because of the fact that, as mentioned earlier, PageRank 4 doesn't actually mean 4.00. It could be PageRank 4.12. And a PageRank of 3 could actually be a PageRank of 3.98. Imagine how easy it might be, if yours was 4.12 and your competitor's was 3.98, for your competitor to overtake you and beat your PageRank.

So, while it's always good to have a higher PageRank than those of all of your competitors' PageRanks, being two points ahead really means you are "at least one point ahead".

The reverse is also true. Your PageRank of 4 might actually be 4.96 and your competitor's PageRank of 3 might actually be 3.07. That gap would be difficult for your competitor to close, especially if they weren't committed to their web presence and you were committed to yours.

Still, you cannot know exactly what your PageRank is relative to your competitor, so you need to actively keep ahead. I always recommend aiming for a two-point lead. That way you know you're at least 1 point ahead. At the same time, you don't want to invest every dime you have in having a HUGE lead on your competitors. You just need to be ahead and stay ahead.

To help you get a feel for where your competitors might be relative to your PageRank, it is good to track your progress every week. Whole integer fluctuations give you a clue that a PageRank might be close to the higher of the two numbers. For example, if your competitor's home page PageRank dropped from 6 to 5, you know it is probably only slightly below 6 for a while at least, so expect it to pop back above 6 soon, which will happen if they decide to focus on it.

The image in Figure 22 shows a week-by-week tracking of the PageRanks of a fictitious company and two of its competitors. The integer jump (e.g. going from 4 to 5) gives a visual clue as to what the number might be close to.

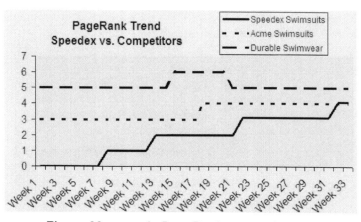

Figure 22 - sample PageRank comparison report

61.Keep a constant track of your competitors'
PageRanks. All else being equal, nudging ahead of them
can have a profound effect on your website traffic.

Diets don't work. Neither do search engine tricks

You might receive advice about building web traffic using tricks to get your search rankings up. Perhaps you were offered tools and services to help you fool search engines into doing your bidding. "Add this tool", they say or "do this to your website now, and lo and behold, you'll shoot to first place, the customers will rush in, and you'll become rich and famous."

I look at these offers the same way I look at fad diets.

Do you know anyone who lost 60 lbs and kept it off? Keeping in good physical shape requires a commitment to healthy behavior over the long term. It's about your everyday lifestyle, not about a problem you fix and forget. When you do get in shape, you become more attractive to people you come in contact with, and keeping in shape offers a lot of other benefits too.

It's the same with Search Engine Optimization; it's about keeping your web presence in premium shape so that it becomes a magnet. That work is manageable, when you do a little of it every day.

> # 62.Commit to adding a little to your website every day. It doesn't have to be a dissertation on world peace. A paragraph or two of new, relevant, valuable information in most cases will be enough to keep content changing and attractive.
>
> If you use a Web Content Management System (see page 45) that allows you to schedule postings across days or weeks, use that feature to make sure at least one new piece of information appears on your website every day.

Hiring someone to tend to your yard

Some of us like to do our own yard work. At the Scanlan household, we try to do it ourselves. Eventually the neglect overwhelms us (because we're busy raising a family and working) and we have to hire professionals to do a big cleanup job on the yard. In our neighborhood, you can easily tell which families hire someone to come every week to do a bit of maintenance and which ones do it themselves. Those that get a little weekly help are in far better shape.

Search Engine Optimization works like that. Your appearance in search engine results will improve if you engage in best practices for the web every single day. What does "best practices for the web" mean? It means two things in particular: (1) adding content to your website every day and (2) searching for opportunities to spread the word by creating Inbound Links to your website.

Adding a blog entry every day

A blog entry must be to the point, succinct, accurate, interesting and valuable. "Valuable" means of value to the reader.

Creating Inbound Links

Regardless of your subject matter, there are forums, bulletin boards and other types of communities focused on subjects ranging from Knitting to Fishing Rods. There are also "generalized" communities like Squidoo.com LinkedIn.com and many, many more. Each welcomes your contribution as long as it provides value to their readers. And most if not all are OK with you including a link back to your website as part of your signature in the blog or forum posting you make. The key here is that your posting must give real value to the reader. The payback to you is the link back to your website which both raises your standing in page rankings and perhaps drives a bit of traffic through the link itself.

While there are optimizations you can apply to your website that will help immediately, the bulk of your search engine progress relies on daily commitment to best practices for the web. These activities are good for business, good for customers and they will attract more and more customers the more you pay attention to it. More and more, Google and other search engines refine their processes to reward such best practices. Search Engine Optimization companies that focus on gaming the system will go out of business, along with their clients that buy into the notion of the SEO equivalent of diet fads.

Give and you shall receive

You are a Subject Matter Expert in your own business. That's why you are running a blog in the first place; because your facts and perspectives are of value to others.

If you make a posting to another high quality, well trafficked blog, (making sure to include your name and link back to your own blog), your contribution to that site will be rewarded in several ways:

- A link back to your site that may drive extra direct traffic to your blog.

- You get your name up in lights where many people may see it.

- This high-quality Inbound Link will often add to your rankings among search engines.

> # 63. Take the time to make well-written, valuable postings to other websites, and include a link back to your own website inside the posting. Usually, it is a question of adding a comment to someone else's blog posting; sometimes you can create an entire blog posting.

Don't be afraid to "give away value" in this manner. You can still post the same text to your own blog of course, and that should remain your greatest focus, but it is better that you make the posting of your own creation and expertise rather that someone plagiarizing your work on another blog and taking credit for it. It's kind of like "eating your own children before someone else does".

What does Google PageRank mean?

Google PageRank is a number between 0 and 10 that a web page receives from Google. You don't apply for it, buy it or rent it; it's the intellectual property of Google. Calculated automatically from a variety of factors by the Google Corporation, the PageRank for a given web page indirectly effects where in the search results that page will appear. If your web page has a lower PageRank than a competitor's, Keyword matching being equal, your competitor's web page will appear earlier than your web page in the search results. That is, prospects see your competitor's web page before they see yours and are therefore more likely to do business with them than with you.

Having a higher PageRank than your competitor's PageRank is what defines a "good" PageRank, regardless of its absolute value.

A PageRank of 4 is five times more valuable than a PageRank of 3. A PageRank of 5 is five times more valuable than a PageRank of 4, and so on.

There is no "good" or "bad" PageRank in an absolute sense. Your page must be at least equal your competitors' PageRanks. If you sell shoes online, a PageRank of 2 can be enough if your competitors' PageRanks are lower. Higher is always good, of course, but PageRank relative to competitors' PageRanks is what counts when someone searches for the product or service you offer.

The physics of how the web works today has reopened the competition within many established product categories. The dominant player has become vulnerable to smaller players who simply get their act together on the web, and seize the Page One position in search results for their product category.

A PageRank of 4 in one product category might be excellent, while a PageRank of 7 in another product category might be poor. It all depends on what your best PageRank is with respect to a competitor's best PageRank. For example: A PageRank of 7 would be poor for IBM because its competitors' PageRanks, Microsoft™ and Apple™ being two examples, hover around 9. But a PageRank of 7 would be excellent for the Wyoming Fishing Supply Store, because its competitors' PageRanks are around 4.

The PageRanks of the businesses within a given product category reflect the relative leadership positions of its members.

Let's say you are in the "Business Intelligence Solutions for the Mid-Size Market" product category. All that really matters is what your best PageRank is relative to the other players in that product category. You don't really compete with IBM, so it doesn't matter what their PageRanks are.

What is the "Google Golden Triangle"?

Figure 23 - the Google Golden Triangle

When your website does not appear in the first few lines of the first page – that is, in the top left hand corner of the "white area" on the first page of search results – the person requesting the search is significantly less likely to arrive at your website. That top left hand corner of the white area on the first page of search results is called the "Google Golden Triangle", illustrated in Figure 23.

The shaded areas – those areas to the right and often to the top – are called *inorganic* results, meaning the items listed there display because someone paid money to put them there.

The outlined triangle is the Google Golden Triangle.

The white area is the organic results area. Items display there because search engines calculated they have the highest likelihood of matching what the search person is looking for and they probably have a high PageRank.

Outside the Google Golden Triangle, your chance of receiving the visitor at your website drops to about 10% – that is – one tenth of what it would be inside the Triangle. In addition, when your website's earliest appearance is beyond Page One of search results, your chance of receiving the web visit drops by another 90%.

This makes it imperative for businesses to do whatever they can to get their website to appear on the first page of search results.

"Widgetbait"

Widgetbait means embedding a link to your own site in a piece of software that others are likely to place on the web. That way, your count of Inbound Links can increase dramatically and automatically without you having to create them manually.

"Black Hat" is the term for "gaming" the search engines into giving a web page a higher search page position than it might otherwise deserve.

WidgetBait is a Black Hat activity.

I could ask the question another way: "When you trick search engines by hiding links to your site in pieces of software you distribute for free, (in an effort to raise your PageRank), do search engines frown upon it?" The answer is Yes.

Burying web links in software you distribute as a way to increase the number of Inbound Links to your site, is a method used by companies to fool search engines into thinking a website is more significant that it is. You see, websites with many links pointing to them, one might reasonably argue, are more popular, better known and well trafficked. That usually is the case, but WidgetBait breaks that model.

Here are several reasons for not engaging in Black Hat activity to increase your position in search engine results:

1.   Any activity that tries to raise search result position but does not add customer/visitor value attracts the attention of Google and other search engines because such activities devalue search results. Search engines have been known to take action to negate its effect.

2.   Your website will not accurately reflect the "big picture" you painted out there by adding all those Inbound Links.

Search Engine Optimization is about best practices. Best practices means adding customer value in a repeatable, scalable way, and not through finding loopholes in the system and taking advantage of them.

As Sean Connery said in the movie Family Business, *if you can't do the time, don't do the crime.*

Trust but verify. Check your status every week

There are three big indicators that tell you a lot about the effectiveness of your web strategy.

- The page number of the search results that your web page appears on. (most important)
- The Google PageRank of the two or three most important pages on your website.
- The raw number of Inbound Links to your website.

Keep a log in a spreadsheet with a chart to illustrate the trend over time.

Grammar, spelling, punctuation and good language

"Quality is Job 1"

Everyone makes grammatical errors once in a while and it will serve you well to fix typos (typographical errors), punctuation, spelling and grammatical errors in your posting. It is "easy on the eye" (my dear mother's phrase for a handsome man) to read well punctuated, properly spelled text. And it will keep your reader engaged. That's what you want, right? To keep your reader interested so he or she will continue reading from your blog.

> # 64.Take the time to pore over your blog posting for grammatical errors and misspellings before you hit the <post> button. If your blog application allows you to revisit old posts, consider rereading older posts for opportunities to update them with new information.

Here are some tips on writing good English in blog postings that make blog postings easy to read:

- A paragraph is a container for an idea or a point you are making. When, for example, you go from talking about how to assemble a fishing rod kit to how to filet a fish, start a new paragraph. Examine any magazine article and see how a good author will start a new paragraph when he or she moves to a new idea.

- Capitalization: Begin sentences with a capital letter. Although your reader may see a period at the end of the previous sentence, a missing capitalization makes them work. A capital letter reinforces structure and makes it easier to continue reading.

- Brevity: When four words will say the same as six words, use four words. That is according to George Orwell. (See George's material below).

- The fancy English that might have earned you an A+ on a school essay, often serves in a blog to make something sound more complicated than it needs to. Keep it simple.

- Three short sentences, one long one, three short sentences, one long one, and so on. The three short sentences build background for the one long sentence and makes text easier to read; it builds a rhythm that your readers will appreciate, even if they never notice it consciously.
Example: "It was a warm day. The goose packed her handbag. The hen took her purse. Between the two of them, they would spend the next four days crossing the big desert, leaving the security of the farm behind them forever".

Take your time. Writing good English is worth the effort. Everything you write on the web might be around long after you are dead, so when your grandchildren read it, you want them to be proud of you. And if poor English is good enough, you're probably wasting your time making the posting in the first place.

Go back later and edit. A night's sleep can sharpen your eye for errors. If you have the ability to re-edit old postings, go back and revisit them when you have spare time.

George Orwell's writing tips[4]:

A scrupulous writer, in every sentence that he writes, will ask himself at least four questions, thus:

1. What am I trying to say?

2. What words will express it?

3. What image or idiom will make it clearer?

4. Is this image fresh enough to have an effect?

---

[4] From Orwell's essay "Politics and the English Language"

And he will probably ask himself two more:

Could I put it more shortly?

Have I said anything that is avoidably ugly?

Never use a metaphor, simile, or other figure of speech which you are used to seeing in print.

Never use a long word where a short one will do.

If it is possible to cut a word out, always cut it out.

Never use the passive where you can use the active. (Example: "*My homework was eaten by the dog*" versus "*The dog ate my homework*", respectively).

Never use a foreign phrase, a scientific word, or a jargon word if you can think of an everyday English equivalent.

Break any of these rules sooner than say anything outright barbarous.

Jerry Pournelle's advice

Go away and write a million words. That's actually about a half dozen novels or more. That's a lot of writing, but will give you the practice you need.

Forget about shortcuts to becoming a writer. Writing classes, Writing for Dummies, (even this blog entry) are all fine and dandy, but *practice* is what you need.

Stay topical and stick to your blog subject

Years ago, I asked an expert this question: "How can a blog get lots of traffic?"

He answered: "Make a posting to it every day, make sure each posting is on the same subject, and that the content is valuable to the visitor. After a year of that dedication, you might notice traffic picking up."

When you make an entry in your Fishing blog about Knitting, you fail to reinforce your position for relevant content for Fishing. It's like selling a knitting kit in a fishing tackle store. You waste space, confuse visitors and offer little value. Just like physical stores, people won't come to your fishing blog to read about knitting. In fact, for those who do come to read about fishing, an off-subject blog entry is an invitation to depart.

Bloggers get distracted. They start off their exciting new blog with some great material on their subject and before you know it, they're talking about their vacation in Scotland and how they cured their Athlete's Foot using fried haggis.

65. Don't talk about the weather, unless you're posting to a weather related blog or website. Every sentence in every blog posting must relate to the subject of the blog posting. Revisit a few of your old postings and remove any irrelevant sentences. Keep everything on your website strictly on subject.

Subject matter density increases your chances of getting displayed early in search result, but more importantly, it keeps your reader focused. Stick to your subject, post every day and stay with topics that visitors are interested in today.

For example, if your blog is a political pundit site, when the Presidential Primaries are on, talk about them. When the presidential election is on, talk about that.

PageRank not WebsiteRank

I've been asked the question "Hey, Liam! How do I raise the PageRank of my website?"

My answer is "You don't. You raise the PageRank of a *page* on your website".

I oversimplify. There is some connection between the respective PageRanks of pages within a website – pages on a website can influence each other's PageRank – but each page gets its own PageRank.

If you'd like to test the assumption that different pages on the same website get different PageRanks, install Google Toolbar, which has PageRank bar on it, into your browser and visit www.ibm.com. (See Figure 24 for illustration of Google PageRank displayed by the Google Toolbar). The Google Toolbar will show you that the page you are taken to has a whopping PageRank of 9. No surprise there; it is IBM after all. Then click your way round their website and you will see PageRank values all the way down to zero, depending on which page within www.ibm.com you visit.

66. Install Google Toolbar into your browser. It's free and it displays the PageRank of the page you are currently viewing in your browser. Search Google for it and follow the instructions for installation.

Figure 24 - PageRank is displayed in the Google Toolbar

Why is the fact that each page has its own PageRank so important, versus every website having its own PageRank?

Search results are returned as a *list of pages* not a list of websites. When your business appears in search results, it is a *single page* of your website that is listed. Multiple pages from your website can be listed of course – and a happy thing it is when it happens – but each page appears as a discrete item in the search results. For success in search results, all you really need is for your business to appear at least once on Page One of search results. You could say that all you need is to have one page, the right page, on your website with a high PageRank and, well, forget about the rest of the pages, as far as search results are concerned.

It is usually better to have one page with a PageRank of 6 than 500 pages with a PageRank of 4.

67.Consider each page of your website to be a discrete target for Search Engine Optimization. If you are a small organization, for example a 2-person reflexology service, pick two or three pages on your website to focus on for SEO.

One page might relate to the reflexology service itself, another might be about the products you sell related to it, and the third page might contain customer testimonials. Your blog, also on your website, will regularly point to those three pages, and any external links to your website will also point directly to one of those pages, not to your home page. (More detail on this subject in the next section).

Focus link attention on high value posts

Not all blog posts are equal, and you might wish certain of them to get more attention than others.

Where it makes sense and is sensitive to the context, create a link from other, less valuable blog postings on your blog to a post on your blog that you know is of greater value to visitors. This has the effect of increasing the likelihood search engines will favor that higher value blog posting when displaying search results.

68.Feed those web pages that work.
You're four months into your SEO project. You've been diligent adding a blog posting almost every day, and if you've had Google Analytics in your website from the beginning, so you know where your traffic is coming from. Select the two or three pages with the highest traffic coming from search engines (not from Inbound Links). Google Analytics will list the traffic that comes as a result of people searching. Examine your older postings and wherever possible, create a link back to these two or three blog postings.

Keep killer posts for busy days

I don't know why, but Tuesday always seemed to be the busiest day of the week on any website traffic report I have even been able to observe. Thursdays were in second place for some reason. Perhaps people slacked off Mondays and Fridays and cruised a bit on Wednesdays.

Your killer blog post

If you've come up with the Cure for the Common Cold and wish to post it to your blog, don't publish it on a Saturday. Post it on Monday at about 8pm New York time. When the search engines comb the web for new stuff, your new post will be picked up and broadcast to all those who are getting a feed on the search for common cold cures. More people read their feed on Tuesday morning than any other day of the week, especially Saturday or Sunday.

The other thing to remember is that highly topical posts will get a better hit rate than stale or premature posts. For example, if you wrote an epic essay on Barack Obama's family journey to the United States and wish to post it to your blog, a good time to post it is the night before Barack is likely to feature heavily in the news.

For example, he will compete in the Pennsylvania Primary with Hillary Clinton on April 22, 2008. Many folks will be searching using his name on that day. Ideally, you want search engines to have picked up the arrival of your very fresh essay about him the day before. That way, your chances of receiving traffic are at their highest.

> # 69.Post the strongest blog entries Monday afternoon and Wednesday afternoon (to get picked up by search engines for the next day). Post weaker blog entries to appear on Saturdays and Sundays. If you only have time for two blog postings per week, Tuesdays and Thursdays are usually the days when most Internet browsing is done, so consider Mondays and Wednesdays as the ideal days to make the posts.

Is there a quick way to determine my search results page?

Not that I know of specifically, but I don't worry so much if a page appears beyond about 100. This is because, in the higher numbers, a huge jump can take place in a short space of time. For example, a page could appear on Page 231 on one day and drop to Page 79 within a few weeks, simply because a few good Inbound Links were added to the web for that page, or page titles were corrected, and Google gave the page a slightly better ranking.

Still, if you really want to track the exact page number your web page appears on, start where you found it last time and work backwards. (This assumes you are making positive progress week to week). In other words, if you found it on page 121 of search results last week, start searching on page 121 this week, then page 120, 119, etc., until you find it.

It's more difficult to go from Page 4 to Page 2 of search results than it is to go from Page 104 to Page 102. That is because there is usually more competition in the lower page numbers as companies who put a modicum of effort into SEO can probably appear in the top ten pages easily. To get to Page 2 means that you are probably competing with people who are putting meaningful effort into their Search Engine Optimization efforts.

So, consider any valid number up to 100, or maybe even only 40 or 50. That way, when you chart your progress, the scale of your chart (0 to 50) allows you to see movements in the single digits.

> # 70.Know and track your progress in search results.
> Play the role of a prospect looking for the product or service you offer. Enter the Keywords they might typically enter – remember: they don't know you, so your company or product name can't be used for the search – and take a note of your website's first appearance in the displayed search results. Perform this test on the same day every week – with the exact same search words – and record the result as "page.line". In other words, if your website appears first as the third item on page 7 of search results, log the appearance as 7.3. The trend over weeks will show your progress.

Always reply to any question to your blog

There is nothing more valuable than when others take the time to post to your blog. Honor that investment by responding with a thorough answer when it happens. A question from an outsider, coupled with a valuable answer is exactly the kind of magnet for people looking for an answer to a similar question in the future.

I've often gone searching for an answer in Google only to be pointed to someone's blog where the answer was thoroughly answered. For example, if I search for "how to create a table in Microsoft Word" in Google, one of the results (with a PageRank of 4 by the way) on the first page told me exactly how to do it.

If there is a spelling mistake or grammatical error in the question, consider fixing that also. Good spelling and grammar are more likely to be used to search later than exact misspellings.

- Answer questions promptly, thoroughly and accurately.
- Fix any spelling or grammatical errors in the question (if your blog provider lets you do that).
- Use a graphic to illustrate the answer if it helps.

Spell out any provisos, like "this solution works for Microsoft Word for Windows 2003" (in case it might not work on other versions). That will at least help the reader understand why your solution might not work everywhere.

71.As soon as you can, respond to every comment on your website. Many CMS (Content Management Systems) provide a built-in mechanism for visitors to add comments. A comment is routed through a designated email address for verification. You get an email to which you can respond Accept/Reject/Edit.
If you do not have a CMS system, provide a way for your visitors to communicate with you. Even a basic link to your email address will help collect good feedback from your website visitors.

Good luck!

About the Author

Liam Scanlan was born in 1960 in Dublin, Ireland. He left his home country in 1983 and had the wonderful opportunity to travel the world with his employer, Nixdorf Computer, in the heady days of minicomputers.

In 1989, he finally settled in the United States, working for Microsoft for five years before starting a series of companies, among which was the founding of Bocada in 1999. Bocada reached eight million dollars in revenue and through its 75 talented employees, served customers the world over. Before Bocada, Scanlan developed, shipped and sold numerous software and hardware products, including the 1995 release of one of the first web traffic analytics tools on the market.

He lives today with his wife and three children in Seattle, Washington, and makes his living mostly through search engine optimization consulting services and speaking engagements. He can be contacted at liam.scanlan@gmail.com or through his comments and questions page: www.foreverup.com/bm/magnet